Tips and Traps When Buying a Home

Other McGraw-Hill Books by Robert Irwin

Tips and Traps When Buying a Home

Robert Irwin

Third Edition

McGraw-Hill

New York Chicago San Francisco Lisbon London
Madrid Mexico City Milan New Delhi San Juan
Seoul Singapore Sydney Toronto

ISBN 0-07-141829-6

This book contains the author's opinions. Some material in this book may be affected by changes in the law (or changes in interpretations of the law) or changes in market conditions since the manuscript was prepared. Therefore, the accuracy and completeness of the information contained in this book and the opinions based on it cannot be guaranteed. Neither the author nor the publisher is engaged in rendering investment, legal, tax, accounting, or other similar professional services. If these services are required, the reader should obtain them from a competent professional. The publisher and the author hereby specifically disclaim any liability for loss incurred as a consequence of following any advice or applying information presented in this book.

This book is printed on recycled, acid-free paper containg a minimum of 50% recycled, de-inked fiber.

McGraw-Hill books are available at special discounts to use as premiums and sales promotions, or for use in corporate training programs. For more information, please write to the Director of Special Sales, Professional Publishing, McGraw-Hill, Two Penn Plaza, New York, NY 10121-2298. Or contact your local bookstore.

Contents

Preface

Welcome to the brand new, third edition of this first of the "Tips &
Traps" series. When I wrote the first edition, I had no idea how
wildly popular this book (and this series) would become (millions
have been sold). Apparently, a book with actual practical (not theo-
retical) advice on buying and investing in real estate was long
needed in the field and, I'm delighted to see, is still well received.

This new edition has been completely rewritten and updated.
While I've retained some of the classic examples, many are new
(such as how to flip properties) and specially suited to today's market. If you're new to real estate, or are even a veteran who wants to
get up to speed, I think you'll find this book a wise guide.

Good luck in your real estate ventures!

Robert Irwin

1
Should I Buy a Home?

Are you ready to make the home-buying commitment?

There are lots of pros and cons revolving around buying a home versus renting one. The old advice that home buying always pays off is no longer automatic in all parts of the country and for some people.

Rent or Buy?

You should rent:

- If you don't want the bother of home maintenance and repair
- If rental rates in your area are low (compared to home prices)
- If you plan on moving around a lot because of job or other commitments

You should buy:

- If you want to take advantage of (recently very high) equity appreciation
- If you want the interest and tax write-off from a home
- If you want added security and privacy

While you can spend a lot of time debating the rent versus own question, my suggestion is that if you're even remotely interested in a home purchase, you at least move forward enough to find out what you can afford. After all, you can always opt out to stay/become a tenant.

Can I Afford to Buy a Home?

Once the decision to investigate buying has been broached, it becomes a matter of determining what you can afford. To find out, most prospective home buyers usually begin the traditional task of putting together a budget of their income and expenses. Their two big questions are, "How much money will I have to put toward a monthly payment? How much money do I need for a down payment and closing costs?" Unfortunately, this is like putting the cart in front of the horse.

My suggestion is to stop, take a deep breath, and rethink. What your budget tells you at this stage is moot. Today it all comes down to what the lender says you can afford—how big a mortgage the lender is willing to give you. (It could be for 100 percent of the purchase price!) After all, you can always borrow *less* than a lender's maximum (to reduce your monthly payment, for example). But, it's very hard to borrow *more*.

If you bought a home in the past, say ten years ago, it may seem odd to go to a lender first, before you even do your own budgeting. But be aware that the process of buying a home has changed. Today your budget needs to come later. Your first questions should be, "How big a loan (and monthly payment) can I get?" For that information, you must contact a lender directly.

TRAP—DON'T RELY ON
SECONDHAND INFORMATION

You can only get the answer to how big a loan and monthly payment a lender will offer from a lender. Don't make the mistake of thinking you can fill out a quiz in a book, go through some formulas, and get that information. Neither I nor any other author can realistically tell you what you can afford without knowing your specific financial information and without submitting that to a lender.

Therefore your first step is an easy one. You find a lender and get "pre-approved." (This is something you will need to do in any event in order to get home financing, so it's not a wasted or extra step.)

Pre-approval takes perhaps a half an hour or so of your time. You contact a lender or mortgage broker (see where to find them in Chapter 4), fill out an application, provide some documentation, and that's it. It might cost you $35 for a credit report (or it might not, depending on how good your lender/mortgage broker is), but that's really a very small investment. You'll have your answer in a few days or less.

What Does Pre-approval Do for Me?

You'll find out how big a monthly payment you can qualify for, the maximum size of a mortgage you can afford, and what size down payment you'll need. (If you even need a down payment—in many cases no-down financing is available; see Chapter 4!)

TIP—GET A COMMITED "PRE-APPROVAL" LETTER

Today virtually all lenders will take a look at your credit history, your income, and your assets and then, based on underwriting standards, issue you a "pre-approval" letter. It will typically state the biggest monthly payment their computers say you can afford. If they've actually gotten a credit report on you, checked with your employer, and looked at your bank statements, this is a pre-approval commitment that you can "take to the bank."

TRAP—BEWARE OF BEING SIMPLY "QUALIFIED"

On the other hand, a mortgage broker or even a real estate agent can ask you a couple of financial questions over the phone and then send you a "pre-approval" letter. However, if your credit report wasn't checked, if your income and assets weren't verified, if underwriting standards weren't applied (and if it wasn't issued directly by a reputable lender), it probably isn't worth the paper it's written on. The reason is simple; no lender will back it up.

Can I Rely on What the Lender Says?

Yes.

And no.

Yes, in the sense that today lenders use highly sophisticated computer models based on hundreds of thousands of actual case histories to determine what makes a successful borrower. Where you fit in that financial profile determines the maximum amount that you can borrow. And if you fit the profile of a successful borrower, chances are excellent that you will be one. On the other hand, if you fit the profile of someone who's likely to lose the property to foreclosure, then you might reconsider renting.

However, the one thing the computer and the modeling and the profiling can't tell you is how big a monthly payment (and how big a mortgage and price) will be within your comfort level. For example, the computer may spit out that you can afford a $3000 monthly payment. But, you know from experience that making a house payment of more than $1500 would keep you from sleeping at night. Who's right? You or the computer?

TIP—STRETCHING MAKES SENSE
IN AN "UP" MARKET

If you are looking at homes after having been out of the market for quite some time, you've probably run into "sticker shock." The prices for today's home can be much, much higher than you paid for your old castle. However, your income may have increased sufficiently to handle the new price/payments. Further, even if you have to stretch to make the payments, if the market is moving up, it might be worthwhile. In a rising market, the value of your new home, and your equity, will quickly grow.

Try a Reality Check

Okay, *now* it's time to take a realistic look at your budget. What can you really afford?

It's not hard. Just calculate your total spendable monthly income. That's what you get after taxes, alimony, and other amounts are taken out. Now subtract what the computer says you can afford monthly and see what's left. Can you really live on that for a month?

TIP—DON'T FORGET TO FACTOR IN TAX AND INTEREST DEDUCTIONS

Remember, you can deduct the interest on your mortgage (up to very high limits) and your property taxes from your ordinary income. By adjusting your W-4 form with your employer, you can factor this in and get a higher monthly take-home paycheck. Be sure to ask your accountant.

Your Reality Check

Take home pay (after increasing for mortgage interest and property tax deductions) $_____

Monthly payment (including taxes and insurance) as determined by the lender $_____

What's left for you? $_____

Few people want to radically change their lifestyle in order to buy a home. Those with long memories will recall families in the 1970s who bought homes and then sat on the floor inside because they couldn't afford furniture. Nobody wants to be in that position. So be realistic with the numbers.

Take a few minutes to determine what your actual monthly living expenses are. Don't forget medicines, entertainment, eating out, and so on. On the other hand, for a home that might bring you strong appreciation (read profit) in the future, you might very well want to give up trying to live a princely lifestyle. What you need to decide is what you can live without, and what you absolutely must have. Here's a chart to help you figure it out.

Budgeting to Determine How Big a Payment You Can Afford

Income

$_____$ Net*

$_____$ Increase after calculation for interest and property tax deductions

$_____$ Increase after eliminating voluntary deductions

Less Expenses

$_____$ Utilities (Gas, electric, water, garbage)

$_____$ Phone

$_____$ Cable/Satellite TV

$_____$ Auto (Lease/Purchase pmt., ins., gas)

$_____$ Food

$_____$ Entertainment

$_____$ Clothing

$_____$ Child Care

$_____$ Tuition (private schools)-

$_____$ Maintenance (gardening, painting, etc.)

$_____$ Repairs

$_____$ Child Support/Alimony

$_____$ Medical (services, drugs)

$_____$ Recreation (gym, sports, etc.)

$_____$ Unpaid credit card debt**

$_____$ Long-term loans

$_____$ Total

$_____$ Income Available for Mortgage Payment

*It's important to remember that your net monthly income is after voluntary deductions such as 401K contributions, which can be reduced or eliminated. Also remember, some of your involuntary deductions, such as for taxes, should be reduced because of the deduction you'll get for home mortgage interest and taxes, thus increasing your take-home pay. (See Chapter 2.)

**Unpaid credit card debt is the worst type of liability because it's paid back at extraordinarily high interest rates. Try to pay this down or refinance it into long-term debt before moving to make a home purchase. Lots of credit card debt may cause lenders to reject you for a mortgage.

Add up all of those monthly items you *must have.* Now compare the total to "what's left for you" after making your house payment, as determined earlier.

Reality Check 2

What's left for me $_____

What I must have to live on $_____

If "What's left for you" is bigger, congratulations. The lender's computer was right and you can easily make those monthly payments!

If "What you must have to live on" is bigger, whoa! You'll either have to tighten your belt more, or you'll have to reduce your monthly payment, cut back on the size of your mortgage, and purchase a smaller house. Or reconsider renting.

Life Is Making Choices

You still have other options. In later chapters we'll see how to get sellers to reduce their price. We'll look at mortgages that require nothing down, indeed, that even pay some of your closing costs! We'll see how to rent-to-buy. And more!

Nevertheless, at some point you'll have to return to the above comparison and one way or the other, make "What's left for me to live on" fit under, "What I must have to live on."

You might want to come back to this chapter several times as you go through this book learning different tips and traps when buying and make the comparison anew. Remain confident, however. Almost everyone eventually decides to go forward and buy a home, once they know the trick of how to go about getting it.

2

How to Get a Good Deal in Rising or Falling Markets

Buy in the winter months.

There are good and bad times of the year to buy, and there are good markets and bad markets.

If you can, probably the best time of the year to buy your home is in December, preferably during the last two weeks of the month when everyone is fussing about the holidays.

Historically, there are fewer home sales between Thanksgiving and New Year's (by a wide margin) than any other time of the year, simply because fewer buyers are out looking. Most buyers get involved with the holidays and put off home searching until after the New Year. The last few weeks of December traditionally have the poorest sales of all.

Most sellers who haven't been able to sell their homes during the summer months feel the same way and remove them from the market after Thanksgiving. Often the only sellers who keep their homes up for sale (or list them at this time) are those who are desperate to get out. And if they haven't sold by the end of December, those sellers are very desperate, indeed.

There are so few buyers at the end of the year, in fact, that "motivated" sellers will often grab at ridiculously low offers just to get out of their property. If you want to save money, that's when you should make your offer. Buy your home in late December.

TIP—BUY AND SELL AT THE PEAK TIMES OF THE YEAR

Buy in the winter months, and then sell in the spring and early summer to maximize your profit.

TRAP—BEWARE OF HOT MARKETS

During the very hot markets of the first years of this century, prices and sales continued to rise even at year's end!

Try to avoid buying in late spring and early summer, specifically the months of April, May, and June. Historically, 30 to 40 percent of all homes (new and resales) will be sold during those three months. They are the peak selling times.

A big reason that April, May, and June are such good sales months has to do with school schedules. The school year is ending and families with children feel it is an optimum time to make a move. Also, families tend to be more financially optimistic in the spring and more willing to take the big step involved in a home purchase. Finally, it also has to do with appearance. After the cold and/or wet winter, houses tend to look fresher and more appealing in spring. (Sellers, of course, know this and spruce up their places even more to lure buyers.)

If you want to pay top dollar, join the throngs of buyers and purchase in spring and early summer. Otherwise, wait until the cold of December when you'll usually have better prices.

What If It's a Seller's Market?

A rising market is often called a "seller's market." The reason is simple: There are many more buyers than sellers. Thus, the seller can raise prices and dictate terms—hence a "seller's market."

One characteristic of a seller's market is that homes sell very quickly. This is measured by how long they are listed for sale, before actually selling. If listed homes are selling in less than 30 days, it's a sign of a seller's market.

Another characteristic of a seller's market is that there will be low inventories. Inventory means how many homes are for sale and how long it would take to sell all those that are listed. Normally there will be around a six-month or longer inventory of homes in any given area. When that number dips below two or three months, it suggests a sellers market.

Also check the direction of inventory change. Is the inventory growing, or falling? A falling inventory is another indicator of a seller's market.

TIP—GET THE BEST INFORMATION

 To find out how quickly homes are selling and what the current inventory is your area, you should check with your local real estate board. You can contact any member agent who should be able to readily get the information for you. Or you can simply call them—their number is in the phone book under "Board of Realtors®" and they should either be able to give you the information, or refer you to an agent who can get it for you.

Finally, keep a lookout for prices. In a seller's market, prices will rise. As soon as you see them going up, it may be a good idea to jump in. Never be afraid of the early days of a seller's market. Keep in mind that even though prices may be somewhat higher today than last year, they'll probably be even higher next year. If prices are going up, the home you buy today will be worth even more next year and, hopefully, more still the year after that. You want to catch and ride the wave.

How Do I Know When the Market Has Peaked?—The Seven-Year Cycle

After there's been a seller's market for awhile, the news commentators on TV, the radio, and in print will sometimes begin talking about a "real estate bubble." They will begin forecasting that the market, which may have gone up for a few years, is ready to crash. They may speak of a "real estate bubble" about to burst.

Keep in mind that historically, real estate has tended to go up, and then go down, very roughly in seven-year cycles. If you're early into seven years of up, it's less likely the market will go "bust." On the other hand, if you're late into the seven-year cycle, the market may be ready to swing the other way.

Here's some things you should know about real estate turnarounds:

When Real Estate Bubbles Form and Burst

- Real estate very rarely "explodes" upward in value or "crashes" downward. In other words, there are seldom any true "bubbles." When prices go up, they tend to go up over time as each price increase builds on the last. When they turn down, many sellers convert their properties to rentals, take their homes off the market, or make other arrangements. Rather than crash, the market tends to slow down and prices slowly drift lower.

- The media tends to exaggerate the market's direction, whether up or down. If the market has been high for awhile, expect the media to construct a "bubble" that it will say is ready to burst. If it's been low for a time, expect the media to see "trends" of upward movement. Just because the media announces it, that doesn't make it true.

- Look at the affordability index for the country and your state. The National Association of Realtors (*www.realtor.org*) offers a national affordability index. It tells you how much house the median income family can afford. Whenever the index is over 100, it usually means housing is still fairly affordable, no matter what the media says. When it's below 100, watch out. Housing may have become unaffordable and the market likely will be forced to slow down. Also check newspapers, which usually report affordability indices for your state and local area.

- Check interest rates. The real estate market is very interest rate sensitive. The reason is that most people get large mortgages, and interest rates affect their monthly payments. When interest rates are low or dropping, it means more people will be able to afford bigger mortgages, and consequently, more expensive houses, causing prices to rise. When interest rates are rising, the opposite is true. The real estate market rarely turns down when interest rates are falling. It rarely maintains high levels of sales when interest rates are rising.

- Be aware of housing shortages. Some parts of the country, for example, Southern California, have experienced large influxes of people. However, at the same time, housing starts have been low. The result is a housing shortage. You can usually tell when there's a housing shortage in your area because rental rates will be going up at the same time as interest rates decline. When interest rates decline, tenants buy and become owners, usually causing a flood of rentals that cause rental rates to drop. When rental rates stay up during low interest times, it indicates a housing shortage, which should eventually lead to increasing prices.

- Watch for the "seven-year" cycle. While a very rough gauge, real estate tends to move up, and down, in seven-year cycles.

What If It Turns Into a "Buyer's Market?"

A buyer's market occurs when there are more sellers than buyers. It's characterized by buyer's being able to dictate terms and price to sellers.

If homes are taking longer and longer to sell (often six months or more), it's indicative of a buyer's market. If the inventory (the number of listed but unsold homes) is six months or more and increasing, it's also indicative of a buyer's market. Again, check with your local real estate board for statistics in your area.

If you buy when prices are going down, a buyer's market, you may initially think you're getting a great deal. However, later on you may find you can't sell for what you paid. (Millions of Americans found themselves in this unfortunate position during the real estate recession of the mid 1990s.) You may discover that after commission and closing costs, it will cost money out of pocket to sell!

TRAP—DON'T GET "UPSIDE DOWN"

 This is real estate jargon that means that it will cost you more to sell your house (after paying off your mortgage, closing costs, and commission) than your house is worth.

The trouble with a declining real estate market is that you don't know, and no one can tell you, how far it will fall before it reaches bottom and rebounds. If you buy on the way down, you will lose.

Therefore, if the market is declining; instead of buying, you may want to rent, at least temporarily. While renting doesn't offer all the benefits of ownership, it does allow you to move out gracefully without having to sell at a loss.

Should I Rent Instead of Buy in a Falling Market?

In a falling market there is negative price appreciation. Then the costs of home ownership often more than exceed the benefits. In a down market, you can often rent a home for far less than it costs monthly to buy that same home. (In some areas, a house that costs an owner $2000 a month for mortgage payment, taxes, insurance, and maintenance can be rented for just about half to three-fourths of that amount—$1000 to $1500.)

In short, unless your property appreciates (increases annually in value), from a strictly dollars-and-sense perspective, you may be better off renting temporarily until the market turns around and prices turn up.

What Should I Do Right Now?

Today, instead of deciding to buy or not to buy, take a few moments to analyze the market. Check with your local real estate board, as noted above, about inventories and how quickly homes are selling. Check out home affordability. Look at interest rates. Learn about housing shortages. Investigate the market *before* you make your move.

Don't let personal factors influence your investment decision. For many of us, our purchase decision is made strictly with regard to our personal situation, without considering the market. For example:

Reasons to Buy Without Considering the Market

- You've finally saved up enough money for a down payment.
- You need a bigger house to accommodate a growing family.

- You've moved into an area because of a job change and want a place to live.
- You've received an increase in salary and can now afford bigger home payments.

All of these are excellent reasons to buy a house, but it could be a mistake to act only on them. None of these reasons takes into consideration the housing market.

Buying a home is not like buying a refrigerator or even a car. You expect those items to decline in value as you use and enjoy them. But a home is also an investment, probably your biggest. You should look forward to your home going *up* in value over time.

Therefore, beyond your personal motivation for buying, you must also consider the market.

TRAP—ASK YOURSELF IF YOU SHOULD RENT

 Before you commit to a home purchase, ask yourself again if renting, at least temporarily, doesn't make more sense given market conditions? Only buy when buying makes more sense than renting.

Can I Really Do This?

Keep in mind that all real estate markets are regional. That means that while the market may be up in California, it could be down in Michigan. Down in Massachusetts, up in Arkansas. If you've only got one house to buy, national statistics don't make too much difference. It's only the market in your area that counts.

And it's only you who can decide if now is the right time to buy. If you've got to make a housing choice, then give yourself every chance of it being an educated decision. Don't simply say, "Prices are too high to buy." They may be even higher next year and the year after.

Don't simply say, "This house is cheap because it's selling for less than it did a year ago." It may be worth far less a year from now—and the year after, worth even less.

Look at the facts. To reiterate, check out all of the following:

Checklist for Determining Market Conditions

Are interest rates low or high, rising or falling?_____
Are housing inventories high and rising, low and falling?_____
Are listing times getting shorter or longer?_____
Are their housing shortages in your area?_____
Can more (or fewer) people afford to buy in your_____ area?
Where are you today in the "seven-year cycle?"_____

And always keep in mind Will Roger's famous quip about real estate, "They ain't makin' any more of it!" Even if you guess wrong and buy in a down market, if you can just hang on long enough, chances are you'll come out smelling like a rose. The long-term prospects for real estate are rosy.

3

Choosing Between a Single-Family Home, Condo, or Co-op

For many people, there is no choice to make. They simply want a single-family house and nothing else will do. Others demand a condo or co-op and will not consider an alternative.

Most people, however, at least consider their options. If homes are expensive, will a condo/co-op be cheaper? Will prices appreciate (or drop) faster in a condo/co-op than a single-family house? Are there any real differences?

Price Appreciation in Condos versus Single-Family Homes

Going back about 50 years, the rule of thumb was that when prices went up, condos were the last to appreciate. When prices fell, they were the first to go down. That's changed.

Today, in many parts of the country, condominium price appreciation is faster than for single-family homes. Indeed, in many areas condos sell quicker and for more money per square foot than their single-family counterparts.

TRAP—GETTING THE RIGHT COMPARISON

 Always compare apples with apples. When comparing prices between condos and single-family homes, do it on a square foot basis. If a 2000-square-foot house is selling for $300,000 and a 1500-square-foot condo is selling for $250,000, which costs more for what you get? The answer is the condo! The condo is selling for $167 a square foot, the home for $150 a square foot. It's something to consider.

The reason condos are appreciating faster now than in the past is mainly because there are fewer of them available. Thirty years ago, builders swarmed to condominium construction and conversion. (A conversion is where an apartment building is converted to condominiums.) For the builders, the costs were less for multiple family dwellings, yet the prices they could get were handsome. So they built condos.

Then came the lawsuits. As it turned out, builders had grabbed hold of the tail of a tiger. When the roof on one or two units leaked, the HOA (Home Owners Association) often demanded that the entire roof over all the units be replaced before leaks could appear elsewhere. When the ground settled, the HOA sometimes demanded that the whole building(s) be lifted and a new foundation poured. Similar problems were found with plumbing, electrical, mold—all matter of things. Since the builders often had to guarantee the construction for as long as 10 years (in some cases by state law), they were faced with enormous liability.

Some builders went out of business. Others took the heavy financial hit. But very few built more condos. In California, as an example, in 1999 there were roughly 20,000 new condo units built. By 2002 that number had dropped to roughly 2000.

As a result, in many areas there is a shortage of condominiums. And, consequently, the price of those available is driven higher.

TRAP—WHEN OLDER MAY BE BETTER

When buying a condo, it's best to look for units that are at least 10 years old and that don't have any pending lawsuits. Chances are that any construction problems will have already been taken care of. And you probably won't have as big a risk of being assessed if the existing lawsuits go against the homeowners.

What Is a Condo?

A condominium, as most buyers know, involves shared ownership. You end up with a deed to the property (called a "fee simple") and separately own the inside of the unit while sharing with the other owners the grounds, walkways, and recreational facilities—in short, everything outside.

Another way to look at it is as if you were renting an apartment and then decided to buy your rental unit. (Indeed, some condos are converted apartment houses.)

It's sometimes useful to know that there are actually two separate kinds of condominium ownership. The first is the one with which most people are familiar—you could be on the fifth floor of a building and you own only that airspace that your unit occupies.

The second is called a townhouse (technically known as a PUD, or planned unit development). Here units are not arranged on top of one another. Rather, you own the ground underneath your unit and the airspace above.

TRAP—TOWNHOUSES ARE DIFFERENT, BUT NOT THAT DIFFERENT!

Don't make the mistake of thinking a townhouse is legally different from a condo. In terms of ownership, it's not. Rather, the difference is in the layout. In a conventional condo, you only own an airspace. In a townhouse, you own the ground underneath and the air above.

What Is a Co-op?

A co-op is a cooperatively owned property. This is different from condominium ownership. In a co-op, as an individual you don't actually own any separate airspace or ground. Rather, you own a share of stock in a company, which owns the entire property. While you have the exclusive right to use a particular unit, you don't actually own it in the sense of being able to sell it directly. To sell your unit, you must sell your share in the company.

What Are the Pros and Cons of Condo versus Co-op Living?

It's important to understand the ownership difference between a condo and a co-op. With a condo you get title to the property; you actually own airspace (or in the case of a townhouse, the ground beneath and air above as well). You get a fee simple or absolute title.

With a co-op you do not get title to any real estate. Indeed, you do not own the real estate; the corporation does. With a co-op you get stock in the corporation that owns the real estate, and that stock entitles you to a proprietary lease on a specified apartment from the corporation. You're a stockholder and a tenant, not a property owner.

While up until very recently, condo owners were the last to take advantage of real estate boom periods; not so with many co-op owners. Most of the big gains occurred when an apartment building located in an urban area (such as Manhattan) was converted to co-op status. The first to buy (often the former tenants) saw huge increases when they resold, in large part because of the shortage of available rentals. They bought an apartment in a city where just finding any place to live could be a problem.

Another factor has been timing. Most of the co-ops were established a good many years ago before the big price hikes in real estate that occurred in the late 1970s, the late 1980s, and once again in the late 1990s and early 2000s. If you bought prior to any of these market bumps, you would stand to see a big increase in value, regardless of the type of real estate. For those who bought co-ops in urban areas where there were already housing shortages (as noted above), the increases were even more dramatic.

On the other hand, there are some problems with co-op ownership not found with condos. First of all, there are the finances. By its very nature a co-op tends to be less financially stable than a condo. Remember, when you buy into a condo, you own your unit. If you can't make the payments on your mortgage, you lose, not the other owners. (They only lose the fees that you would otherwise pay toward the upkeep of the common areas.)

With a co-op, however, an underlying mortgage is typically held by the corporation on the overall structure. That means that if you can't make your monthly payments to cover your portion of the mortgage debt, the other owners must make up what you can't pay in order to meet the monthly mortgage payment. The same holds true for property taxes and insurance. If too many owners can't pay, then the remainder might not be able to make up the difference and the entire project could conceivably go into foreclosure.

In short, with a co-op it is very much like an extended family with brothers, sisters, aunts, and uncles all living in close approximation and all contributing to the living expenses. When one (or more) loses a job or gets sick and can't contribute their share, the others must make it up. If they can't make it up, they could lose their home.

The inherent financial instability is the reason that good co-ops are very careful about whom they will allow to buy stock. They want to be sure that any new owners are financially strong.

TRAP—PUT YOUR BEST FOOT FORWARD WHEN BUYING A CO-OP

When buying into a co-op, expect to have a meeting before the board in which you will have to show why you would be financially capable of being a good owner. Although discrimination based on gender, race, ethnic background, medical problems, or other similar concerns is prohibited, nonetheless, some boards have discriminated. Thus buying and later reselling your unit is potentially made harder.

Further, in some parts of the country, such as west of the Mississippi, getting financing to buy a co-op can be difficult. Lenders are concerned about the financial structure noted above, and they are simply not as familiar with the financing as with condos.

What Are the Pros and Cons of Condo/Co-ops versus Single-Family Homes?

When you buy into a shared ownership property (either condo or co-op), you are actually trading off a portion of your privacy in exchange for other benefits such as guaranteed maintenance, architectural control, and amenities such as a pool, spa, rec room, tennis courts, clubhouse, and occasional parties that go along with condominium living.

Shared versus Private Ownership

Pros of Owning a Single-Family House
- You are generally "master of your domain"
- Increased privacy
- No monthly owner fees paid to the HOA or board
- Strong price appreciation in good markets

Cons of Owning a Single-Family House
- Generally more expensive on an absolute cost basis
- Maintenance required
- Little architectural control

Pros of Owning a Condo/Co-op
- Little or no exterior maintenance or repair
- Amenities such as pool or clubhouse
- Strict architectural control
- Sometimes utilities and insurance are paid for by HOA
- Recently stronger price appreciation in good markets
- Often more security

Cons of Owning a Condo/Co-op
- Little say about the exterior of your unit
- Noisier

- Generally smaller units that single-family homes
- In a natural disaster (earthquake, hurricane) you could lose everything
- Historically slower price appreciation

A shared property is often the choice of those who are looking for a first or a retirement house. The shared living means others are around to help out, the financing is usually similar as for a single-family house, and sometimes you can get into a good location for less (although on a square footage basis, you may also be getting less). Many first-time buyers purchase a condo or co-op and then live in it a few years, building up their equities. When they sell, they have a small nest egg that they can then apply towards a house. Many retirees opt for a condo/co-op because they don't want to mow lawns anymore and are concerned about security.

TRAP—DO YOUR HOMEWORK ON A CONDO

If you buy into a condo/co-op, expect to spend some time on the homeowner association (or board of directors) just for self-protection. If you don't, you'll find that the HOA or board is always doing something that you consider ridiculous and that you don't like. If you're an owner, you'll want to be a part of decisions that affect your home and its value. On the other hand, be aware of HOA burnout. This comes after you've been a member of the board for a year or two and found that you can't get done what you want to get done. Often, owners will get discouraged and will then sell their unit. If you're at least aware of this possibility, you may be less inclined to make such a drastic move when a stalemate does occur.

As an additional resource on this topic, check into *Tips and Traps When Buying a Condo, Co-op, or Townhouse,* McGraw-Hill, Irwin, 2000.

4

How to Get a Lender to Put Up All or Most of the Money

Nothing-down financing—does it really exist? Or is it just a buzz-word used by real estate gurus selling you a seat in a seminar or a tape on late-night TV?

Today, it really does exist, for some buyers.

And that's a good thing, too. Most people who want to buy a home often find that the biggest roadblock is coming up with the cash down payment. (So if you're feeling the pinch, rest assured you're not alone!)

Let's face it; we live in a credit society. A family with a $100,000 annual income can easily obtain a new car loan with almost nothing down and a $500-a-month car payment. But that same family may not have $5000 in the bank in a savings account. In fact, over 70 percent of all families have little or no cash savings. (On the other hand, that other 30 percent or so have whopping big savings accounts!)

What Your Mortgage Payment Includes

- Interest on your loan
- Return of equity (principal)
- Hazard insurance (if you put down less than 20 percent)
- Taxes (if you put down less than 20 percent)

I'm reminded of that old saw about the two investors who want to buy the Empire State Building in New York. The first investor, just returned from a meeting with the sellers, tells the second, "I've got good news and bad. The good news is that they'll take our $100 million offer." "Great," says the second investor. "What's the bad news?" "They want $500 cash down!"

Where Do I Find a Good Lender?

Before you get a good loan, you must get a good lender. These days they are everywhere. You can go to a single-source lender such as your bank or your credit union. Or a multiple-source lender such as a mortgage broker.

The mortgage broker has the advantage because he or she solicits loans from a wide variety of lenders, including banks, insurance companies, and pools of investors. Often a mortgage broker can match you up with just the right lender for your needs.

Ask your real estate agent for a mortgage broker recommendation. Also, check with any friends, relatives, or associates who recently bought a home. Chances are they used a mortgage broker and can recommend (or steer you away from!) a mortgage broker. As a last resort they are listed in the yellow pages under Mortgage Brokers. (Note: A mortgage *banker* may not make loans directly to consumers. Look for a mortgage *broker.*)

Also consider online mortgage brokers. Check a good search engine for them. Also, look into:

www.eloan.com

www.quicken.com

www.lendingtree.com

Will a Lender Give Me 100 Percent of the Purchase Price?

Just a few years ago the "standard" down payment on a home was 20 percent. That's $40,000 on a $200,000 property, a lot of money for most people.

Today, however, with new financing available from Fannie Mae and Freddie Mac (the "big brothers" of financing who buy most of the loans that lenders and others make on the secondary market), that's all changed. Today you can easily get financing for 90 percent of your purchase. Depending on your financial situation, you may be able to get 100 percent, sometimes even 103 percent of financing (to help pay for some of your closing costs)! These are called "conforming" loans. (They conform to Fannie Mae and Freddie Mac underwriting standards.)

Is there a catch?

Of course there is! You have to meet specific guidelines set up by the two giant secondary lenders. Generally speaking these guidelines are as follows:

Underwriting Guidelines for "Big Brothers:" Fannie Mae and Freddie Mac Loans

- Maximum loan amount (as of this writing) is $322,700
- Must meet strict credit guidelines including a strong FICO score (see below)
- Must meet strict income guidelines

Where do you get this "miracle" financing? Almost any bank, mortgage broker, or other large lender can handle it for you. (See Chapter 4 for more details on locating a good lender.)

TIP—SPECIAL LOANS FOR SPECIAL BORROWERS

You do not always need to have great credit or high income to qualify for a conforming loan. Both lenders have special programs that are designed for people with limited income and credit problems. For a few examples (available through lenders, not directly from Freddie Mac or Fannie Mae):

- *Affordable Gold®️ 5* from Freddie Mac, is designed for moderate-to-low-income borrowers. It only requires a 5-percent down payment and is available on a mortgage with terms of 15, 20, and 30 years.

- Freddie Mac's, *Affordable Merit Rate® Mortgage* is a mortgage for borrowers who have had some small credit problems. The loan is for a higher interest rate. If the borrower is able to make 24 consecutive on-time payments within a four-year qualifying period, the interest rate is reduced.
- Fannie Mae's *Fannie 97®* offers a 97-percent mortgage. There are, however, income and geographic area restrictions. And the borrower must participate in face-to-face education programs. And there are other restrictions.

Other Low-Down-Payment Mortgages

There are other ways to get financing with little to nothing down. VA (Veterans Administration) guaranteed loans, up to around $240,000, are for nothing down. FHA (Federal Housing Administration) insured loans, up to around $210,000 are for just a little bit down. (See the next chapter for details on these.)

Will I Need Mortgage Insurance for Low-Down-Payment Loans?

Unless you go with a VA loan, the answer is yes. All FHA loans have it. And all conforming loans where the loan amount is greater than 80 percent require it. In other words, on a $100,000 house, if you put less than 20 percent down, you're probably stuck with paying mortgage insurance.

Mortgage insurance does not protect you. It protects the lender. If you don't make your payments and the lender has to foreclose on you, the insurance picks up a substantial portion of any loss the lender may incur. That's why lenders demand it. (That, and the fact that the government requires it!)

TRAP—EXPECT EXTRA CHARGES FOR MORTGAGE INSURANCE

PMI (Private Mortgage Insurance) is expensive. Expect to pay an additional 1/2 percent in interest for it. However, once you pay your loan down (or your property appreciates) so that your mortgage is less than 80 percent of the value of your property, you can usually get it removed.

Be Creative—Have the Seller Handle the Low-Down-Payment Financing for You

What used to be called "creative financing" is nothing more than having the seller finance your purchase. Instead of going to an institution, such as a bank, to get a mortgage, the seller carries back the "paper," sometimes for the entire price.

However, in order for the seller to do this, he or she must have a substantial equity in the property. Often this is the case with retirees who are downsizing. They want to get a smaller home and often have their existing home paid off, or close to it.

While they may need some cash, often they come out of the sale with a lot of extra money, which they then put into the bank or CDs to earn interest. However, if interest rates are low, they are in for a hard time. Until you offer to borrow the money from them as part of the purchase. While the bank may pay 1 to 5 percent, you can easily pay 6 to 10 percent, depending on market conditions. For a seller who is looking for income from cash, you can be a godsend.

Often these seller-financed sales are constructed with two mortgages. You go out and get a conventional first mortgage for up to 80 percent of the sales price. (These are relatively easy to obtain.) Then the seller lends you an additional 10 to 20 percent to cover what otherwise would be your down payment.

Pluses of Seller Financing

- It's almost instantaneous—no waiting for a lender to fund.
- Little qualifying—Most sellers only want to see a credit report showing relatively good credit.
- High LTVs (Loan to Value)—Often a seller will give you the top 5 to 20 percent that would otherwise be your down payment.

Minuses of Seller Financing

- Sometimes hard to find a seller with enough equity who doesn't need to cash out (to buy another property).

> - Sellers may be wary—If you don't make the payments, they
>   would need to foreclose, and their lack of experience and
>   knowledge makes that difficult.

TRAP—LENDER'S RESTRICTIONS

 Much of the "no money down" nonsense that was popu-
larized in real estate in the 1980s involved having sellers
carry back all the down payment. The sellers were
placed at a real disadvantage in terms of collateral.
Today, with a hot market, few sellers will do this. In addition, institutional lenders may restrict their mortgage
amount unless you put down at least some of your own
money.

Other Sources for the Down Payment

It would be nice if we could simply write out a check for the down
payment, if we can't get 100-percent financing. However, most of us
are always pressed for cash. Other than a flush checking or savings
account, here are some sources of cash for a down payment that you
may not have considered before.

Alternative Possible Sources of Down Payment

- Cash value of life insurance (borrowing on it may be inadvis-
  able—check with your financial advisor first)
- Refinancing or selling an auto or boat
- Sale of other physical assets to generate cash
- Sale of stocks, bonds, or other securities (first check with your
  financial advisor)
- Sale of present home
- Gifts or loans from relatives or friends

- Refinancing investment real estate you already own (should be done before applying for the new loan)
- Income tax refund
- Letter of credit or credit line from a bank (should be obtained before applying for the loan)
- MasterCard, Visa, or other credit card (should be obtained before applying for the loan)
- "Sweat equity"—offering to fix up a house in return for a reduced down payment
- Accumulation of funds from your regular income between date of purchase and close of escrow (insist on a long escrow—three months or more)
- Personal loan on hobby materials, jewelry or furs, cameras, or other property.

TRAP—BEWARE WHEN BORROWING THE DOWN PAYMENT

Many of the sources of cash listed involve borrowing. However, many loan programs restrict the borrowing of funds for a down. (Not all—some Fannie Mae and Freddie Mac programs specifically allow it.) Be sure to check with what your lender requires. If you do borrow your down payment, it's a good idea to borrow it at least three months before you enter into a transaction to purchase a home. That way, you'll have the cash in hand and borrowing will show up as an existing loan against your credit, not new borrowing specifically for the home, which could disqualify you.

It's important to be aware that an extra loan against your credit could decrease the amount you could borrow on a home. (You will be tying up some of your income to pay off that loan. That income won't be available to help you qualify for a home mortgage.)

Don't Overlook the Closing Costs

Many buyers simply forget about this very real cost. Don't. Closing costs are expensive. Typically they are around 5 to 8 percent of the purchase price of the house. If you pay $100,000 for a home, expect to pay about $5000 to $8000 in closing costs.

These are cash costs. You'll need to come up with them *in addition* to your down payment. (We'll have more to say about them in Chapter 16.) They include:

Typical Closing Costs When Purchasing a Home

- Points (percentage of the mortgage paid to the lender to compensate for a lower interest rate)
- Title and escrow charges
- Other lender and escrow fees
- Attorney fees

Reducing or Eliminating the Closing Costs

It's possible to get your closing costs reduced, eliminated, or deferred. One method is to have your mortgage amount increased to cover the closing costs. You are getting a $100,000 mortgage with $5000 in closing costs. This is converted to a $105,000 mortgage with no closing costs. Check with your lender to see if it can be done.

Another option is to have the lender roll the closing costs into the loan. You end up with a slightly higher interest rate (around 3/8 percent more), but the lender covers your loan costs. You are getting a $100,000 mortgage with $5000 in closing costs at 6 percent interest. This is converted to a $100,000 mortgage with no closing costs at 6 3/8 percent. Again, check with a lender.

Yet another option is to negotiate the closing costs with the seller before you commit to the purchase. Remember, closing costs are negotiable. You and the seller can agree between yourselves who will pay them. As part of the deal, the seller can agree to pay all or part of your closing costs for you.

TRAP—WHY SHOULD A SELLER PAY YOUR COSTS?

 What are the chances of a seller agreeing to pay your closing costs? Pretty good in a buyer's market where the seller is desperate to unload a house. Not so good in a seller's market where houses are moving rapidly. Also, keep in mind that negotiability extends to all areas of the transaction. If you're getting a terrific price, the seller is less inclined to pay part or all of your closing costs. On the other hand, if you're giving the seller pretty much what he or she wants in price and the market isn't too tight, then reduced closing costs may be possible.

Yes, You Can!

In today's highly sophisticated mortgage market, you often can get a lender to cover all or most of your down payment, even all or most of your closing costs. And, as we've seen, when the lender won't do it, there's always the possibility of having the seller carry back paper to cover your down and costs.

But you may finally be wondering, what if I'm not such a qualified buyer? What if my credit is just so-so? What if my income is a bit short? All this in addition to my not having the money for a down payment.

There's still hope. Sometimes lenders will give you a mortgage but increase the interest rate to justify the increased risk to them. Sometimes sellers simply won't care.

And there's always the chance you can find a house that has an old mortgage on it (usually FHA or VA) that you can assume with no qualifying at all.

In today's market, almost no one who wants to buy a home goes away empty handed. Look into the next chapter to find a good lender.

5
Get the Best
Mortgage in Town

One of the newest and most important developments in real estate lending is that now almost everyone can get financing, from the most- to the least-qualified buyers.

In the past, in order to get a mortgage you had to be a premium buyer—high salary, few other debts, cash in the bank, and sterling credit. Not so anymore. Lenders are taking less-qualified buyers and offering them financing with slightly higher interest rates to make up for the added risk. In other words, if you've been shy of applying for a mortgage because of some credit problems, give it a try. You could be surprised at the positive results. Of course, if you're that prime buyer, you'll get the lowest interest rates and the best terms.

The Lowest-Interest-Rate Hunt

For most people, the first consideration with regard to a mortgage is the interest rate. Higher interest rates translate into higher payments; lower rates, lower payments. Consequently, most people want the lowest interest rates possible.

TIP—SHOP LENDERS, NOT MORTGAGES

If you have a credit blemish or have trouble otherwise qualifying, shop for a lender, not an interest rate. Some lenders specialize in borrowers with problems; others won't touch them.

TRAP—BE CAREFUL WHEN COMPARING MORTGAGES

 The best way to compare interest rates is to do it for *like-kind* mortgages. You don't want to compare apples and oranges. Today there are two major kinds of conventional (nongovernment insured or guaranteed) mortgages available: a fixed-rate mortgage, where the interest rate does not change for the life of the loan; and a variable-rate mortgage, where the interest rate can change. When you compare mortgages, be sure you compare fixed-rate to fixed-rate and variable to variable. (There are so many different varieties of variable-rate mortgages that comparing them is really very difficult.) Of course, at some point, you'll also want to compare variable with fixed, but that's a much more complex calculation, as we'll see shortly.

How to Compare New Fixed-Rate Mortgages

Each lender who offers fixed-rate mortgages posts its current interest rate. These rates are often printed weekly in local papers. They also can change daily. In many areas a newsletter or online service gathers them all up and sends them off to agents.

TRAP—WHEN INTEREST RATES ARE LOW, LOCK THEM IN

 Variable interest rate mortgages always offer lower rates. But the variable rate will rise when the interest rate market goes up. It's usually better to lock in a fixed-rate mortgage when the interest rate market is low, rather than to try for an extra point or so by getting a variable rate.

There are also numerous online lenders such as *eloan.com* and *mortgage.com* that post their current interest rates. These are very easy to check simply by going to their Web site. Major online services such as *MSN.com* and *AOL.com* will also lead you to mortgage rate postings.

But best of all, if you check with a mortgage broker who handles dozens of lenders, he or she can quickly tell you the best rate in town for the specific amount and type of loan you're hunting for.

Making the Fixed-Rate Comparison

Here's what a typical list of lender might look like:

LENDER	INTEREST RATE	POINTS	FEES
Associated Lenders	6.7	0	0
ABC S&L	6.4	1.5	1,400
Amalgamated Bank	6.3	.5	700
Jones Bankers	6.2	2.5	1,350
WW S&L 7	6.1	3.0	1,200

What's the best loan? It's the best combination of interest rates, points, and fees. In the previous example, Amalgamated's loan is outstanding because of the low interest rate, low points, and few fees, even though Jones and WW offer a lower interest rate.

At first glance, this list of interest rates might seem complex. After all, there isn't just an interest rate. There are also *points* and *fees*. What's that all about?

What Are Points?

A point is a single percentage of a mortgage. Thus two points on a $100,000 loan equals $2000; four points equals $4000, and so forth.

Points are a trade-off the lender is making. If you want a lower-interest-rate loan (lower than the market), you can get it, if you're willing to pay points. The more points you pay, the lower the interest rate will be.

On the other hand, since points are cash out of your pocket, you may be willing to accept a higher interest rate. The higher the rate, the fewer the points. Normally, at zero points, you're paying the market rate.

Note: The interest rate is very important since it will help determine your monthly payment. The higher the interest rate, the higher your payment. The lower the interest rate, the lower your payment.

What Are Mortgage Fees?

Another charge is *loan fees*. These can be almost any amount, from nothing (where the fees are absorbed into a higher loan amount or higher interest rate) to many thousands of dollars. While some lenders are very up front about telling you what these fees are, some sneak them in at the last moment.

When the loan fees are actual costs, such as for an appraisal or credit report, they are considered justified. However, when they are simply added on to give the lender a better "yield" (total return on the mortgage), they are usually called *garbage fees*. We'll have more to say about them in Chapter 16.

If you are primarily interested in the lowest monthly payment and have some cash on hand, look for the lowest interest rates. However, be aware that lenders with low interest rates often make up for it by jacking up the points and fees. It may cost you more to get the loan.

On the other hand, if you want to reduce your closing costs and can stand a bit higher monthly payment, look for a lender who charges few to no closing costs and points. You'll usually pay a higher interest rate, but you won't have to come up with as much cash out of pocket.

TRAP—SWITCH LENDERS

In all cases, if the interest rate or closing costs are unreasonably high, seek another lender. But do this when you first apply, so you have time to change. If you wait until the deal is ready to close, it may be too late to go hunting for a new lender.

TIP—YOU CAN TRADE CLOSING COSTS FOR INTEREST RATES

Many lenders today will allow you to trade closing costs and points for interest rates. They'll even have a scale. As the interest rate goes up, the closing and points go down and vice versa. See the previous comparison. Be sure you compare lenders. Sometimes you'll find that the trade-offs are too steep from one lender and much more reasonable from another.

How to Compare Variable-Rate Mortgages

Variable-rate, also called *adjustable-rate,* mortgages (ARMs) can also be compared, except that many more factors are involved. The first thing you'll notice is that the interest rates usually will seem much lower for ARMs than for fixed-rate loans. Once again, don't be fooled. Remember, compare apples with apples, not with oranges.

The low initial interest rate (often called the *teaser*) is the traditional appeal of ARMs. As such, they appear to be giving you a better deal. But it isn't necessarily so.

There are a number of different factors to take into account when comparing variable/adjustable-rate mortgages. We'll cover six of the most important:

- Teaser rate
- Caps
- Indices
- Margin
- Adjustment period
- Steps

What Is a Teaser Rate?

Most ARMs have a low beginning interest rate. This is usually only a teaser, a come-on to get you to sign up for the ARM. Often the teaser is several percentage points below the true rate. What this means is that in the first few adjustment periods, your effective interest rate will rise even if interest rates in general do not!

As an example, the discounted teaser rate may be 4 percent and the true market rate may be 7. You get the ARM at 4 percent. However, if it has 3-month adjustment periods with a maximum adjustment of 1 percent in interest each period, within 9 months it will be up to 7 percent. Your interest rate will go up 1 percent the first 3-month period, 1 percent the second 3-month period, and 1 percent the third 3-month period, so that 9 months after you get the loan you are paying 7 percent instead of 4.

Additionally, some of these loans are written in such a way that the interest rate will continue on up to make up for the below-market interest rate you received as part of the teaser. So your interest rate could continue on up beyond 7 percent for a time!

Remember, the teaser rate is only temporary. Don't be fooled into thinking that it is the true rate of your mortgage. Ask the lender what the true rate is. You'll be shown the APR (annual percentage rate), which will be higher than the teaser but probably still not as high as the current market rate of the mortgage (because the APR is a blending of the teaser and the current mortgage rate).

When comparing ARMs, it's usually to your advantage to go for the one where the teaser *lasts the longest,* thus maximizing your period of low interest rates.

What Are Caps?

Adjustable rates often have caps limiting the maximum amount that the interest rate can rise over the term of the loan and the adjustment period. Rate caps prevent the interest rate on a variable rate mortgage from rising indefinitely.

Some loans offer *payment caps,* where the amount the monthly payment can rise (to compensate for a rising interest rate) is also capped. It sounds like a good idea, but in reality it can be a trap. Monthly payment caps often lead to *negative amortization,* which, simply put, means that you end up owing more than you originally borrowed!

Negative amortization happens when the interest rate goes up and your monthly payment does not. In this case, each month you may not be paying enough to meet just the interest on the mortgage, let alone repaying the principal.

The excess interest is then added to the principal and you end up paying more than you originally borrowed! (Usually the lender cannot increase the principal of the mortgage over 125 percent of its original amount through negative amortization.)

What Are Steps?

Steps are the maximum amount the interest rate can rise (or fall) during any one adjustment period. For example, a 1.5 step means that the maximum the interest rate can vary during the adjustment period is 1.5 percent. Generally speaking, most borrowers prefer shorter steps when interest rates are rising.

However, if the steps are too short to fully accommodate the market's interest rate increase, many loans provide that the excess can be carried over to the next adjustment period.

What's an Adjustment Period?

This is the time between which rate adjustments can be made. Adjustment periods vary between a short of one month and a long of three years or more. Generally speaking, most borrowers like a longer adjustment period when rates are rising, a shorter one when they are falling.

For example, a summary of different lenders caps might look like this:

Comparing ARMs

Lender	Interest rate	Steps	Adjustment period	CAP
AVD S&L	5.00	1	6 months	5
Mary's Bank	4.50	2	3 months	6
Long City S&L	3.78	1	monthly	8

For AVD S&L, the teaser rate is 5 percent. It can rise 1 percent every six-month adjustment period with a cap of 5 percent to a total of 10 percent.

For Mary's Bank the teaser rate is a lower 4.5 percent. However, it can rise faster—2 percent every three-month adjustment period with a 6-percent cap to a total of 10.5 percent.

Long City S&L offers the lowest teaser, 3.78 percent. However, the rate can rise the fastest, 1 percent every month up to a maximum increase of 8-percent cap, or a total interest rate of nearly 12 percent.

Note that while Long City S&L appears to have the lowest interest rate, because of the short adjustment period, that rate can rise faster than any of the other lenders who apparently have higher teaser rates, but longer adjustment periods.

TRAP—IT'S NOT JUST TEASERS

Be careful not to look at just the teaser rate. Check also the steps, adjustment period, and the caps. These all help to determine how fast the interest rate, and consequently the monthly payments, on the loan can go up.

TIP—COMPARE ALL THE FACTORS

In addition to a low teaser, in general you want to avoid payment caps and look for the lowest interest rate cap combined with the shortest steps and longest adjustment period. This should offer you the lowest cost loan in a rising ineterest rate market.

What Are ARM Indices?

Adjustable-rate mortgages are all tied to an independent (of the lender) interest rate index. These indices rise and fall along with other interest rates and, accordingly, so does the rate on your mortgage. Ideally, most borrowers want an interest rate that has the least volatility so your mortgage payment won't bounce around too much. On the other hand, lenders want a more volatile interest rate that more closely corresponds to changes in the market place.

More Commonly Used Indices

- 6-month T-bill rate
- 1-year T-bill rate
- 3-year T-bill rate
- Libor index (London Interbranch rate)
- Cost of funds for the lender
- Average of fixed-rate mortgages
- Average rate paid on jumbo CDs

TIP—IF YOU WANT LESS VOLATILITY

Historically among the least volatile rates have been the cost of funds and the Libor index. However, as we move into new economic climates, that could change. Lenders should provide you with a chart showing changes in the index for your loan. Be sure you ask for a chart that includes the period of 1979 through 1981 and 1999 to 2003 so you can see how the index performed in both high-interest-rate and low-interest-rate economic conditions.

What Is the Margin?

Each adjustable rate has a margin. This is a figure that is added to the index to give you your interest rate. For example, the margin might be 3 percent. Thus, if the index is at 5 percent, add the 3-percent margin and you have your effective mortgage interest rate of 8 percent.

TRAP—IT'S NOT JUST THE INDEX

Keep in mind that the index rate is not your interest rate. The lender's margin is added to the index, and this can increase your effective interest rate substantially.

Plan Your Strategy

If you're going to live in the home only a short time and then resell, get the lowest teaser rate with the longest adjustment periods and shortest steps possible. For example, if you plan to live in the property for only three years, you might be able to find an ARM that gives you a below-market interest rate for the entire period of time!

Also, most people aim for the most stable index. That way you have a better idea of your monthly payments. But if interest rates are falling, you may want a more volatile index that will reflect falling rates in a more rapidly falling monthly payment.

In addition, don't compare just interest rates and points with ARMs. Sometimes an ARM with a higher interest rate and more points is a better deal, if it has a more favorable adjustment period, steps, margin, and so on.

Comparing Adjustable-Rate with Fixed-Rate Mortgages

Now we're at the stage of comparing apples with oranges. However, in truth, a direct one-to-one comparison isn't usually very helpful. Rather, what's more important to most borrowers is comparing the usefulness of each type. It's sort of like saying, "Do I want to eat an orange now, or will an apple taste better?" Here are some guidelines that may prove helpful.

When interest rates are low, get a fixed-rate mortgage to lock in the low rate. When interest rates are high, consider an adjustable-rate mortgage with payments that will fall as interest rates come down.

If you desperately want to buy a home but can't qualify for a fixed-rate mortgage, try an adjustable. The lower teaser rate should make qualifying a bit easier. (Currently lenders qualify not just on the basis of the teaser, but on an average between the market rate and the teaser, which is still probably lower than for a comparable fixed-rate mortgage.)

If you can't afford to have fluctuations in your monthly payment, get a fixed-rate mortgage. You'll at least know what your payments will be every month.

If you plan to sell soon, get an ARM and take advantage of the low teaser rate. But beware, your plans could change unexpectedly!

Sometimes ARMs have lower initial loan costs. If cash is a big consideration for you, look into them. Remember that with an ARM, if interest rates go up, so do your payments. (This may occur even after rates have peaked and started to come down. Because of your adjustment period, you may play "catch-up" for months after the downturn.) You can't call your lender later and say, "I can't handle a $200 increase in my monthly payment!" Your lender isn't going to be sympathetic and will threaten you with foreclosure if you don't pay. The time to consider a big monthly increase is before you get that adjustable-rate mortgage, not afterward.

Fixed- or Variable-Rate Mortgage?

You should get a fixed-rate mortgage:
- If you can lock in a low-interest rate
- If you plan on keeping the property a long time
- If you want a fixed mortgage payment (does not go up or down)

You should get a variable rate mortgage:
- If interest rates are high and you can get a long-term, low initial (teaser) rate
- If you plan on selling or refinancing soon
- If you can handle flexible mortgage payments (that can rise during the life of the loan)

Hybrids: What About a Combination Fixed and Adjustable?

There are a whole bunch of hybrids out there, any one of which may be better for your situation than a straight fixed or ARM mortgage.

What Is a Convertible Mortgage?

Some ARMs may be "convertible" to a fixed rate, or vice versa. Many allow a conversion at a set date—three or seven years, for example—in the future. Just be sure the conversion is guaranteed at the lowest interest rate at the time of conversion.

There are literally hundreds of types of convertible mortgages available. Some lenders will even create one just to suit your financial situation. Be sure to ask.

What About Short-Term Fixed, Amortized over 30 Years?

The whole point behind an ARM, from a lender's perspective, is to give a loan that can respond to interest rate fluctuations. Another way of accomplishing this is to give a shorter-term fixed-rate mortgage.

Currently lenders are offering short-term fixed-rate mortgages in the following time lengths, all amortized over 30 years, 15 years, 10 years, 7 years, 5 years, or 3 years. The shorter the term, the better the interest rate is. What this means is that after the initial period, you have a "balloon," a single large payment where the remaining balance is due.

For example, you can get an interest rate reduction if you agree to get a loan with a balloon in 15 years (see the following). You might get an even bigger reduction if you agree to a balloon in 10 years instead of 15. If you agree to a balloon in 3, you might get the interest rate reduced the most. (*Note:* The monthly payments can still be spread out—amortized—on the basis of 30 years. It's just that you have a shorter due date, or balloon payment at the end.)

TRAP—BEWARE OF THE BIG BALLOON PAYMENT AT THE END

On short-term fixed-rate mortgages, if it turns out that you can't sell or refinance as you planned at the end of the term, you could lose the property to foreclosure! You're gambling a lower interest rate on future market and personal financial conditions. Therefore, make sure a shorter-term mortgage includes an automatic refinancing option at the end. Usually this is an ugly adjustable, but at least if worse comes to worst, you won't be without a loan.

Hybrid mortgages are available from banks, savings institutions, and mortgage brokers—anywhere that you'd get any other type of mortgage. However, your best sources are the mortgage brokers, who deal with many lenders, and thus have a better sense of what's out there.

Balloon or Amortize (Spread Out) Payments?

You should get a balloon mortgage:

- If you plan on reselling or refinancing soon
- If you need a lower interest rate
- If you can lock in a "roll-over" loan to cover the balloon when it comes due

You should get a fully amortized (paid off) mortgage:

- If you want equal payments to fully pay off the loan
- If you plan on keeping the property a long time
- If the risk of a big balloon payment (or having to take out a high-interest roll-over loan) bothers you

---

What About a Fully Amortized 15-Year Mortgage?

Some people simply want a shorter mortgage. As opposed to the hybrids just discussed, in a fully amortized shorter-term mortgage, the payments are higher so it can be fully paid off at the end of, say 15 years. (With a hybrid, you have lower payments, but a balloon at the end—here the mortgage is paid completely.)

The advantage here is much less interest over time. With a 30-year amortized mortgage the total interest is more than twice as much at the same interest rate than with a 15-year fully amortized mortgage! Of course, you may be saying to yourself that this is all well and good—yes, you save more than half the interest. But you probably more than double your payments.

Not quite. The difference in payments between the same 15-year and 30-year mortgages is only about 20 percent. You'll end up paying only about 20 percent more monthly. (Yes, it really does work out that way. It's all in the way mortgages are calculated.)

TRAP—GET THE 30 WHEN YOU WANT THE 15

Many people like the idea of saving interest and, since they currently have enough income, jump to a 15-year mortgage. The problem is the higher monthly payment. What if at some point during the time you're paying back the mortgage, you get ill or lose your job? It's a lot harder to repay a higher monthly payment than a lower one. The solution is to get a 30-year mortgage with no prepayment penalty. (Most modern mortgages don't have penalties for early repayment.) No prepayment penalty means that you can pay a higher monthly payment at any time you want. Thus, you can pay the equivalent of the monthly payment to turn a 30-year loan into a 15. However, if the loan was originally set up as a 30 year, then at any time making that higher payment becomes a hardship, you can drop back to the lower 30-year payment. When things get better, you again pay more. Here, you get the advantage of being able to pay off the mortgage in a short time *if you choose*, but also have the safety of a lower payment if hard times hit.

What About Biweekly Payments?

Popular a few years ago, some biweekly mortgages are still around. Here, instead of paying your mortgage each month, you pay half the monthly amount every other week. The result is that you actually pay an extra month each year. (There are 12 months, but 52 weeks in a year, meaning you would make 26 biweekly payments which equals 13 months.) Over the long haul, that extra month means you end up paying more in principal each year, which means much less interest down the road. This works for either a 30-year or a 15-year mortgage. With a 30-year mortgage, going biweekly can mean paying it off in around 23 years.

The problem with biweekly mortgages is that you can be forever writing checks. Therefore, the only realistic way of handling them is to have the money taken out of your account automatically every two weeks. You can easily set this up yourself at your bank, or for a hefty fee, there are service companies that will do it for you.

Keep in mind, however, that the biweekly mortgage is not for someone who is self-employed and gets paid irregularly. An unstable cash flow can cause real problems when you have a mortgage payment due every other week.

What About FHA or VA Loans?

The government, except in some rare instances, does not lend mortgage money directly to consumers. It does, however, insure or guarantee lenders, who thus are willing to give you a mortgage, oftentimes at better than conventional nongovernment rates.

What Is the FHA Program?

FHA mortgages are insured by the government and are offered through most lenders, such as banks. Generally the down payment is low, under 5 percent. The interest rate, however, is usually competitive with conventional loans. The big problem with FHAs is that the ceiling, or maximum amount for FHA loans, is relatively low. As of this writing it is at $210,000.

If you get a new FHA loan, you'll have to pay the insurance premium for the loan up front. (See the explanation for the similar PMI in the previous chapter.) The premium is fairly high—close to 4 percent of the loan amount. You can, however, add the premium to the loan, although this does increase your monthly payments.

Additionally, you are required to occupy the property as your residence in order to get a low down payment, and the property itself must pass a strict qualifying appraisal.

There are generally no prepayment penalties for FHA mortgages and they are partially assumable. (That means that the buyers must qualify as if they were getting a new FHA loan. However, generally they can assume the sellers' loan at the existing interest rate.)

What Is the Veterans Program?

Some loans are guaranteed by the Veterans Administration. The guarantee is not to you, but to the bank or S&L that makes the loan. These mortgages offer competitive interest rates and, in many cases, no down payments and reduced closing costs.

In order to get a VA loan you must have been on the active list in the armed forces during certain periods of time. (These change periodically—check with the Veterans Administration for the current requirements—*www.va.com*.) In addition, the property must pass a rigorous appraisal. Finally, you must plan to occupy the property.

VA loans are usually nothing down to you, and the seller must pay most of the closing costs. However, as with FHA loans, the maximum amount is relatively low (around $240,000 as of this writing).

Further, in general, they are fully assumable. You can sell the property and the buyers can pick up the loan at the existing interest rate. However, once you get a VA loan, you are on the hook for that loan for as long as it is on the property. Even if at some later date you sell the property, you may still be responsible for the loan! If the future buyer defaults, the VA could come looking to you for repayment! You must get a release of responsibility from the VA at the time someone else buys to fully get off the hook. (But that next buyer must then qualify as a veteran.)

What Is a Graduated-Payment Loan?

Less popular today than in the past, loans with a graduated (instead of fixed) payment can be incorporated with almost any other, including government loans. Generally it means that you pay less when you first get the loan and are least able to pay. Then, presumably as your income goes up, so does the monthly payment.

Don't get a graduated-payment loan unless you're quite certain you're going to have an increase in income. If your income remains the same or declines, you could be in big trouble down the road.

What About Reverse-Equity (Annuity) Mortgages?

After a halting start over a decade ago, reverse-equity mortgages are making a comeback. Designed for senior citizens, they allow you to live in your house and get a monthly stipend from a mortgage you put on it. The amount that you receive is added to the mortgage amount monthly, plus interest. You can stay in the house until you die; then the lender gets the place and can resell. The FHA provides probably the fairest of these mortgages.

TRAP—DON'T GET THROWN OUT

If you're looking at a reverse-equity mortgage, be sure the loan provides that you can live in the property in perpetuity. You wouldn't want to be evicted after a dozen years or so because the mortgage had grown higher than the value of the property or because you had lived longer than expected! Again, check out this feature in an FHA version.

Very few lenders offer reverse-equity loans. Consult with a mortgage broker about possible sources in your area.

Should I Ask the Sellers for a Second Mortgage?

If the sellers are willing, it's probably the best mortgage you can get. There's usually no qualifying and you can bargain for the interest rate. (You might offer a slightly higher purchase price for a lower interest rate.)

Many sellers, however, cannot give a second mortgage because they need to cash out in order to buy another home. Others are reluctant, fearing you might not make the payments and they would have the considerable expense of foreclosing and taking the property back.

You can also get a second mortgage from an institutional lender such as a bank. Here the second mortgage typically has a higher interest rate than the first.

Watch out for "balloon payments" on seconds. This results when the mortgage is not fully amortized—when the monthly payments do not fully pay off the principal. At the end of the term on a seller's second, you could end up owing a substantial amount of money. For example, if you borrow $10,000 at 10 percent, interest only, for 7 years, at the end of the term, you still owe $10,000! (It was *interest only!*)

Of course, seconds can be amortized, or paid off monthly.

However, many seconds have payments that only partially return all the principal. This is frequently the case with a mortgage that is "amortized for 15 years, due in 5," which is similar to the short-term fixed-rate loans discussed earlier.

This means that the monthly payment is high enough to pay back the loan in 15 years. But you owe it all back in 5 years. When the fifth year comes around, you still owe most of your principal. Now you must either dig deep into your pockets or refinance.

What Are Discount Prepayment Mortgages?

More recently entering the market are discount/prepayment loans. These typically offer you a discount on the interest rate or in the form of cash back *if* you agree not to pay off (prepay) the mortgage for a set period of time. For example, the lender may offer you a $1000 discount provided you won't prepay within three years. If, however, for whatever reason you must prepay before the time limit, you are subject to a hefty penalty, sometimes six months' worth of interest.

To many people this sounds great. The lender is paying you when you borrow the mortgage. However, it could be a poor bonus if your fortunes turn and you suddenly need to refinance. If you do, the penalty could hurt. In most cases, there is no penalty if you sell instead of refinance during the prepayment phase of the loan.

TRAP—YOU DON'T ALWAYS GET WHAT YOU PAY FOR

Beware of lenders who offer a very low incentive discount, a very long prepayment period, and a high penalty. You could end up being locked in for five years just to save $500 bucks, with thousands in penalties for prepaying.

Discount/prepayment loans are available from banks and mortgage brokers on most types of mortgages, including both fixed and adjustable.

6

Get Agents Working for You Instead of the Other Way Around

The vast majority of real estate agents are very hardworking people whose goal is to serve you by getting the best home on the market for you. Along the way, however, there are a few agents who are simply incompetent or unscrupulous, or who really don't work very hard at all. Since you're very likely to work with an agent when you buy a home (around 85 to 90 percent of all homes for sale are listed with agents), you need to be sure you get a good one.

Most people think picking real estate agents is like picking apples out of a barrel. There are going to be a few shiny ones here and there, a few bad ones on the bottom, but overall they are going to be pretty much the same. Unfortunately, that's simply not true.

Yes, there are always a few bad apples, but the real distinction has to do not so much with ethics as with ability. Some agents are able to help you, but some are not.

It's important to understand what I mean by "ability." I'm not talking about understanding the laws of your state with regard to the licensing of agents or the selling of real estate. Today, in all states agents must pass strict tests as well as continue their education to make sure they understand what their legal and fiduciary responsibilities are. In this sense, the overwhelming number of agents are capable. It's when it comes to serving your needs that many fall down.

My father, who was a successful agent for more than 30 years, used to say, "When I first got my license, I thought I was ready to sell real estate. It wasn't until 10 years later that I finally learned how to really be an agent." To understand what he meant, it's important to realize just what's involved in being a real estate agent. Once you see the selling of property from the agent's perspective, you may get a whole new view of how to pick the right one.

What's Involved in Being a Good Real Estate Agent?

According to the Hollywood stereotype, the typical real estate agent drives a big Mercedes or at worst a Caddy, Lexus, or BMW. He or she (most agents are women) meets clients over cocktails, attends flashy parties with lenders, and makes oodles of money (often into seven figures, but certainly into six figures).

Recognizing a Good Agent

- He or she always has enough time for you.
- The agent is assertive enough to help you make decisions, but not so aggressive as to try to make decisions for you.
- The agent knows the area "like the back of his or her hand" and specializes just in home sales.
- The agent is experienced and "up to speed" (at least five years actively in the business).
- The agent can provide referrals of recent satisfied home buyers.

The truth is somewhat less exciting. According to several surveys, the average agent in 2000 made under $50,000 a year. In addition, out of that $50,000 the agent paid for a business automobile, gas and maintenance for that car, phone, dress clothes for work, and other expenses involved in operating a business.

In other words, after expenses, the average real estate agent was not a high roller, but pretty middle to low-end in terms of income from real estate!

"How can that be?" I'm sure you're asking. The agents you've met always seemed so successful.

The truth? Often it's mostly a front. A lot of agents simply work hard at looking good.

You also have to understand that real estate is actually a second or part-time career for many individuals. It attracts an enormous number of people who are looking for less than full-time work. Typically these are people who have retired from another profession (teaching, the military, government, or large corporations) and are now on a pension and looking to pick up a few extra bucks.

Often these people have dabbled a little in real estate and are in an office as much to look for bargains for themselves as to service you or other clients. In the trade these people are called "inactive" agents.

The real trouble with inactive agents who have another steady source of income is that they aren't "hungry" enough to get out there, find the really good houses, and negotiate the toughest deals. (After all, whether they make a sale or not they know they'll survive—because of their pension.)

How many "inactive" agents are out there? A lot. The easiest way to tell is to remember the 80/20 rule-of-thumb. Every active real estate broker (and I was one for many years) knows that 20 percent of the agents sell 80 percent of the property. The corollary is that 80 percent of the agents are only selling 20 percent of the property. That big 80 percent includes many of the "inactive" group.

You Want the Hot 20 Percent

Let's talk about that 20 percent that's making the vast majority of deals. These are the "active" agents. Typically they are aggressive, often relatively young individuals who have no means of support other than real estate. To put it bluntly, if they don't make deals, they don't eat.

Three Most Important Questions to Ask Your Agent

1. How long have you been full-time? (Avoid part-time agents or those with less than five years of active experience.)
2. What neighborhoods (or area) do you "farm?" ("Farming" is where agents go door-to-door soliciting listings—they intimately learn the neighborhood, learn when properties are coming up for sale, and can tell you off the top of their head what's available right now.)

3. How much time and effort will you commit to me? (You want someone who will be ready to go whenever you are, phones you regularly with updates, and continually previews properties for you.)

If you were to isolate this group of individuals, you would find that
they typically make over $100,000 a year and probably half make sub-
stantially more. They are out there beating the bushes from dawn til
dusk. They look at *every* new house that comes on the market in their
area. They are constantly "farming" (talking with potential sellers) to
get listings. When they get an offer, they go in there and negotiate all
night if necessary to get the seller to either accept or compromise.
   Is this the agent you want working for you? You bet it is!

How Do I Separate the Active from the Inactive Agents?

You want an active agent. How do you get one? First off, remember
that active agents are *active*.

Identifying the Active Agent

- Has a number of properties listed
- Always working tirelessly, including evenings and weekends
- Extremely familiar with the market in your area
- Ready and able to refer you to numerous buyers from sales they've
  made *in the past few months*
- Busy with real estate (but not too busy to show you houses)

TIP—GET A RESPONSIBLE RECOMMENDATION

A recommendation from a friend is a good method of
finding the active agent. If your friend has had a positive
experience with an agent, it's a good sign. But remember;
it's not a guarantee. Your friend might have just been
lucky and fallen into the perfect house. The agent's efforts
could have been incidental. Even with a recommendation,
you need to be sure you've got an active agent.

Are There Active versus Inactive Offices?

Just as there are two types of agents, there are also two types of offices: the active office where sales are constantly happening, and the inactive office where the agents sit around and commiserate with one another about the slow (to them) real estate market.

There are a few good ways to tell the two types of offices apart:

How to Identify Active from Inactive Offices

- An active office almost advertises heavily. Check the ads in your local paper.
- An active office usually has quite a few agents and they always seem to be scurrying around, not sitting at their desks drinking coffee and reading the newspaper.
- An active office usually has promotions going on to induce greater activity from agents. Walking in, you will often see "salesperson of the month" and "lister of the month" awards—TVs or trips to Hawaii for the best producers of the season, and so on.
- Other agents will know of the active offices and often will speak of them grudgingly as people who are always getting the deals done.
- This is just a personal observation, but I have found that active offices usually have a secretarial staff. The agents are out there selling; the staff handles the paperwork. In an inactive office (without many sales or much revenue), it seems the agents are stuck with all the secretarial duties.

Just keep in mind that the 80/20 rule still applies even in an active office. It's just that in an inactive office, the hot 20 percent aren't there.

How Do I Find an Active Agent in an Active Office?

If you walk in off the street and into an active real estate office (see above), chances are actually against your getting an active agent.

The reason is that all agents pull "floor time." This is time they are expected to sit in the office and pick up potential clients who come in across the transom.

You walk in and you get the current floor agent or, if there's a receptionist, the next agent who is "up." You'll immediately know this person. How? While other people in the office smile at you, this agent will quickly come up, introduce herself or himself, and ask how they can be helpful.

Since almost all agents, active or inactive, are people oriented, they almost certainly will be polite, charming, and apparently helpful. But if they are inactive agents, they could be wasting your time.

TIP—DON'T GET THE AGENT WHO'S "UP"

When you walk into a real estate office cold, don't accept the first agent who comes to see you. Rather, say that you are waiting to see someone, an agent, but you can't remember the name. Now, while the receptionist or the floor agent begins listing the names of the agents in the company, look around the walls of the reception area. As noted, a great many active companies will have "agent of the month" awards hanging there. Very frequently, the award for the past 10 or 12 months will have gone repeatedly to one agent. Just point to the plaque and say, "That's her." Or "That's him." You'll be quickly introduced to the most active agent in the office. If there are no awards to tip you off, then ask to see the broker.

It's important to understand that all real estate offices are organized around one person, the broker. Everyone else is an associate agent. (Even other brokers may have their licenses subordinated to the main broker.)

In a small office, the broker acts as a salesperson. In a larger office, however, the broker typically sits somewhere in a back office and handles closings and other difficult work. In a very large office, the broker frequently may be out making big deals while subordinate brokers handle the day-to-day work.

When you request the broker by name, you are usually asked in response, "Will your name be recognized by our broker?" In other words, do you have an appointment?

Just reply, "My business concerns one of your agents. I want to speak only to the broker." Just the hint that there could be some problem will get you an audience. Real estate companies dread complaints or angry clients. Most will bend over backward to avoid any kind of dissatisfaction.

When you are ushered in to see the broker (or the person who is in charge at the moment in the case of a very large office), carefully explain that you have not yet talked to any agent in the office (thereby avoiding the problem of having one agent or another "claim" you as a client). Tell the broker you are going to be buying a house in the very near future and you want to deal with the most active agent in the office in terms of sales. No one else will do.

The broker may chuckle inwardly at your boldness, but in most cases will tell you who that agent is, and you're on your way. (If the broker refuses, leave. There are almost as many real estate companies to choose from as there are houses for sale!)

Should I Aim for a Large "Franchise" Real Estate Company?

Don't be misled into picking your agent on the basis of the real estate company's name recognition. Over the past few decades, franchising has proliferated the real estate market. But a real estate franchise is no better or worse than a fast-food franchise such as McDonald's or Burger King. All that you are assured of in a fast-food franchise is that you will get no less than a certain quality standard of hamburger and service. The same holds true for real estate franchises.

In most cases, each real estate office, regardless of the franchise name, is individually owned and operated. What you're dealing with is the local broker and agents who have adopted the sign, the coat, and the procedures of a franchising company. However, you still go out with your individual agent to see properties, and it's your agent with whom you'll consult when making an offer.

The franchise office may be no better nor worse than a nonfranchised office in providing you with good, active agents—it does, however, have name recognition, policies and procedures, more advertising clout, and sometimes nicer jackets.

When comparing top agents, I don't feel there's a significant difference. (Some franchises offer their own financing and escrows, which can be a convenience. But in my opinion, it's always better to get your own financing and use an independent escrow.)

On the other hand, if something should go wrong, sometimes it's easier (sometimes harder!) to deal with a franchise company. At least here you know there's a big corporate entity that is concerned with keeping its good name and its customers happy. And it probably has deep pockets.

It's important to remember that real estate, almost more than any other business, is highly personalized. The deal you get will depend mostly on the one person with whom you deal. You can get a great active agent with a nonfranchised company just as well as with a franchised one.

How Do I Help an Agent Help Me?

Once you find an active agent, you must decide whether he or she is right for you. Watch for obvious problems such as personality clashes or basic differences in outlook. In addition, you want to be sure that the agent isn't so aggressive as to overwhelm you. You want to be able to control your agent, not the other way around.

Remember, agents influence your decision by what they do or do not say. Be sure that they aren't using this power to manipulate you into something you may not want.

You will want to be forthright with an agent. Let the agent know your price range. Tell the agent the areas you want to consider. The agent isn't a mind reader and can't find the perfect house for you unless and until you give the agent the parameters of what you're seeking. This doesn't mean you need to tell agents everything about your finances or your intentions, as we'll see shortly. Just offer enough to enable them to work for you.

Should I Work with Several Agents?

It's okay to work with several agents, but only one at a time. Don't hip-hop from one to the next. Only when your relationship peters out and the agent stops showing you properties you want to see should you move on.

Reward a good agent with your loyalty, and the agent will reward you with good work.

When you find that your current agent is no longer productive, try another. But be "up front" with both agents. Tell the second agent the properties you've already seen. Ask the second agent for something new or different to show you. There is a good reason for switching agents over time. First, while the vast majority of properties listed by agents are put on the Multiple Listing Service (MLS), where nearly all agents can work on them, some agents keep really good properties as "vest pocket listings." Other agents won't know about them and, therefore, won't show you the properties. Further, in some areas, companies won't list all of their listings on the MLS. As a result, any one agent may not be able to show you all the properties that are listed.

On the other hand, understand that the agent who first shows you the property you eventually buy may be entitled to a portion of the commission even if a different agent eventually makes the sale. This could cause hard feelings or even problems later on should a different agent submit the offer. Instead of working hard to negotiate the best price and terms for you, the various agents could get into a squabble over who gets what portion of the commission.

Work with only one agent at a time and tell that agent the properties you've already seen and other agents you've worked with. It will save you time and possible problems later on.

TRAP—BEWARE OF THE OVERLY DETERMINED AGENT

 Years ago (before the consumer protection movement was even dreamed of) I knew an agent who had a very aggressive style. He would get his clients in his car, which was connected to his office by two-way radio. (This was before cellular phones.) He would then take them out looking at properties. After he had exhausted his immediate list of properties, he would call his office and ask his secretary to look up other properties to show. Some clients were impressed. They would continue to look until they were exhausted and then ask to be taken back to the office, where their car was located. The agent would refuse! Oh, he wouldn't exactly say, "No!" Instead, he'd tell them about some other house that was just around the corner and was just right for them. He literally kept them prisoner in his car until they finally agreed to make an offer! Of course, they could have always made him stop and then gotten out. But more often than not, the clients were new to the area and had no idea where they were. While some clients did get angry and refuse to consider anything until the agent brought them back, a surprising number actually were coerced into making offers!

Fortunately, such actions today are unheard of. But the story illustrates an important point. Some agents are more actively aggressive than you want or can handle. If that's the case—run, don't walk, away. They'll try to coerce you into making deals you may or may not want.

The Agent's Responsibility Is Not Always to You!

This is a most important point that most buyers simply don't understand. Let's say that you've found an active agent whom you like and with whom you can work. You must now come to grips with the fact that, in many cases, this agent *does not work for you!* He or she is the agent of and works for the seller.

It doesn't matter that your agent shows you around to many houses listed by other agents on the Multiple Listing Service. It doesn't matter that the house you decide to make an offer on has a separate agent who listed it. (This can be confusing to buyers, particularly when very often there is one agent—yours—who shows you a house and takes your offer and another agent—the one who listed the property—who seems to represent the seller.)

Actually, the agent who shows you around may be the "subagent" of the agent who listed the property. In other words, *both* may be the agents of the seller!

TIP—FIND OUT THE AGENT'S FIDUCIARY RELATIONSHIP

 The law of agency in all states is quite clear. It requires that an agent maintain a *fiduciary* relationship with whomever that agent represents. Usually that's the seller. If the "subagent" who's been showing you around takes an offer from you and presents it to a seller, who is represented by a listing agent, both of these people may have a fiduciary relationship, not with you, but with the seller.

What does having a fiduciary relationship mean? It means that the agents owe the seller "integrity, honesty, and loyalty." That translates into the following.

The Effects of Dealing with a Seller's Agent

Unless the seller has authorized it, your seller's agent can't disclose how much less than the selling price the seller might take, even if the agent knows of a specific figure! (This isn't to say that many agents don't hint at the lower figure, but they aren't supposed to come right out and tell you, for example, that the seller said, "My price is $100,000, but I'm so desperate to sell I'd take $75,000, *but don't you dare tell that to any buyer!*")

The agent can't disclose that the seller might accept terms more favorable to you unless the seller has authorized the agent to tell you.

On the other hand, if you tell the agent that you're desperate to buy, that even though you're offering $175,000 you'd be willing to pay $200,000, the agent is *obligated* to tell the seller what you said!

Working with a seller's agent is almost like having an enemy spy in your camp! Of course, in actual practice there is some bending of the rules. And a good agent will always attempt to work fairly with both buyer and seller.

In today's world, where consumers are so litigious, many agents are hesitant to do anything that a seller might construe as violating the fiduciary relationship and that might result in a lawsuit against them. Hence, when you work with a seller's agent (or subagent), don't expect advice on how to get the best terms or price.

TIP—"LOOSE LIPS SINK SHIPS!"

 When you're working with a seller's agent, even one you consider on your side, button you lips. Don't tell the seller's agent the highest you'll go on an offer. Remember the old World War II slogan about loose lips. Don't let the agent know the best terms you'll give the seller. Think of the agent as the seller's earphone. Don't whisper anything that you don't want the seller to hear. Keep your own confidences.

Are There Agents Who Work for *Both* Buyer and Seller?

There is no easy solution to the problem of agency for buyers. One answer, however, that is gaining increasing popularity in some areas of the country is to have a "dual agent." A dual agent represents both buyer and seller. This agent owes both the seller and you, the buyer, "integrity, honesty, and loyalty." However, unless permitted by the seller, the dual agent still *may not tell you if the seller will accept a price less than the property is listed for.* However, to compensate for this, the dual agent may also not tell the seller that you'd be willing to pay more than the price you offer. (The same generally holds true with terms.)

Thus, while the dual agent really isn't 100 percent on your side, the agent also isn't 100 percent on the seller's side either.

Dual Agent versus Buyer's Agent versus Seller's Agent

In a dual agency:
- The agent tries to represent both you and the seller
- The agent tries to avoid telling either party anything that will hurt the other. Usually this means not saying anything that will benefit you

In a buyer's agency:
- The agent represents just you
- The agent must tell you if he or she learns the seller will take less

In a seller's agency:
- The agent represents just the seller
- The agent must tell the seller if he or she learns you are willing to pay more

How Do I Know Whom My Agent is Working For?

Ask.

Your agent is obligated to tell you. Further, before you sign any documents, including a sales offer, your agent should present you with a written statement describing who that agent works for (seller, dual, or buyer). Many states now require a formal disclosure as part of their agency law. (California, for example, requires dual agents to give a signed statement to that effect to both buyer and seller.)

TRAP—GET YOUR AGENT TO DECLARE

Don't assume that just because your agent isn't the listing agent of the property he or she is a "dual" agent. Unless your agent specifies whom he or she is working for, you can probably assume it's the seller.

Should I Work with a Buyer's Agent?

As if it isn't confusing enough already, there is yet another designation of agent we've hinted at, a *buyer's agent*. This is an agent who truly works for you, the buyer. (After all, if sellers can have their agents, why can't buyers?)

There's are some good reasons to work with a buyer's agent. After all, it's the only way you can be sure the agent is on your side. Remember, a true buyer's agent has a fiduciary responsibility to you, not to the seller. Such agents must tell you everything they know about the property and about the seller that's to your advantage, including any information about the seller's willingness to accept a lower price or better terms.

The only problem in dealing with a buyer's agent usually is the fee. If you want a buyer's agent, you sometimes have to pay the commission yourself! (Usually, however, the sellers pick it up.)

At this point I'm sure some buyers are ready to hurl this book out the window. Pay a commission when you buy? In addition to the cost of the house, the down payment, the closing costs, and on and on. Add to that the cost of a buyer's agent's commission?

That's crazy!

Not really. In most cases the seller ends up paying for the buyer's agent anyhow. Buyer's agents are adept at working out the commission with the sellers. The buyer's agent's fee is usually half of a full commission. (If the commission rate in your area is 6 percent, the buyer's agent's commission may be 3 percent.) Often a deal is worked out in which the seller agrees to pay your agent half the commission and the seller's agent the other half.

What About Commissions?

- The commission amount is negotiable, although the average today is around 5 percent.
- When one agent represents the buyer and another the seller, the commission is usually split down the middle.
- The sellers usually pay the full commission.
- The sellers will usually pay your buyer's agent half a commission.
- If the seller's agent refuses to split the commission, you might have to pay your buyer's agent's fee.
- The brokerage takes a percentage of each agent's commission.
- The brokerage may try to impose a "transaction fee" in addition to the commission in order to recover some of its costs—fight this!

Thus, it may cost you no more than if you had worked with a seller's or a dual agent. On the other hand, by working with a buyer's agent, you might save so much on the purchase price that it would be worth your while to pay a commission yourself!

Some areas of the country have many buyer's agents; other areas have almost none. They do advertise in phone books and in newspapers. In addition, regular seller's agents in almost every area know of buyer's agents and usually are willing to at least let you know who they are, if not recommend them to you, once you make it plain that's what you want.

Should you use a buyer's agent?

The vast majority of buyers don't, and that's unfortunate. The only way to get an agent really on your side is to use a buyer's agent. I wholeheartedly suggest you look for one when you get ready to buy.

However, be very wary about signing a buyer's agent agreement. These vary greatly, so have your attorney check it out to see that you don't commit to paying a commission (or a portion of a deposit), or that you can get out of it if the agent proves not be satisfactory.

What About the Bad Apples?

As noted earlier, there are always a few bad apples. (Remember, the vast majority of agents are hard-working people who strive to do a good job and are usually competent.) On the other hand, the bad apples are agents who either are outright crooks or are so unaware of real estate laws that they can cause you harm in a deal. How do you avoid these?

Fortunately, in most cases the bad apples don't last long. After a few deals they often mess up so badly that there are letters of complaint to the state real estate regulatory body, which either revokes their license or disciplines them. The danger is that you might run into one of these bad apples before they get thrown out. How do you protect yourself?

I wish I had a surefire answer. However, the tips here are the same ones that are given when picking any person whom you give your confidence to when it comes to your finances:

Avoiding the Bad Apples

- Find out how long the agents have been in the business. Even if the salesperson has been in business only a few years, the office should have been around a long time. Try to do business only with an agent or office that has a long track record—five years at the least.

■ Work with a national franchisee. While earlier I stressed that this is no guarantee you'll get an active agent, it does give you some assurance of at least minimal quality in terms of procedures. Besides, if the agent should be truly incompetent and negligent, you can always appeal to the national office of the chain.

■ Ask to see the agent's real estate license. In all states, agents *must be licensed,* and that license must be prominently displayed in the agent's office. Agents will be pleased to show it to you.

In truth, most buyers are going to consider only the above three suggestions (plus recommendations of friends). However, if you're really concerned, here are some additional steps you can take to find out about an agent's background:

■ Check with the local better business bureau or (in an extreme case) the local district attorney's office to see if there are now pending or have ever been any complaints against the agent or the office.

■ Call the state real estate department and ask if the agent's license has ever been revoked or suspended or if the agent has ever been disciplined. (This is public information to which you are entitled.)

Quite frankly, few buyers will ever take these last two steps. In most cases, we tend to accept a friendly smile and a solid handshake as evidence of competence and honesty. And in most cases things work out just fine. Remember, however, we are now considering those very few bad apples.

The worst thing that you can do is to find out you've been dealing with a bad agent after something has happened—after you've made an offer that has somehow gone awry and has resulted in a money loss to you or the threat of a lawsuit from the seller or some other injured party. A few calls may suddenly tell you that this agent has been in hot water since she got her license.

Then you'll say to yourself, "If only I had investigated first!" Remember, it takes only one or two phone calls and perhaps 15 minutes of time talking to the right people to get a minimal background check on the person who is going to advise you on what is probably the biggest investment you'll make in your life.

Unfortunately, the truth is that you can seldom be completely sure about an agent (or any other person with whom you deal financially). I recently learned of a very unusual case, an agent who was falsifying loan documents. This person was telling buyers they could obtain financing that they obviously could not qualify for, and was getting it! We'll call him Jim (obviously not his real name).

Jim was securing false verifications of employment (which your employer fills out, giving your salary) and false verifications of deposit (which a bank or an S&L fills out, giving the cash on hand that you have for a down payment). Both these verifications are what a lender bases a loan on. Since most loans today are sold in the secondary market to government agencies, to falsify them can be a federal offense investigated by the Federal Bureau of Investigation or the Treasury Department. Fraud is a serious offense.

Jim was blandly falsifying these documents for buyers, telling them not to worry, it was done every day, it was just a formality, and they'd never have anything to worry about. The interesting thing is that Jim had been falsifying documents successfully for more than three years! He was considered a successful member of the real estate profession.

He might have gone on for more years, but circumstances eventually did him in. As it turned out he was doing more and more deals with more and more people who couldn't really qualify for mortgages, and the lenders never suspected fraud until there was a downturn in the economy. Since in Jim's case the vast majority of mortgages he was placing involved people who were just marginally able to handle the payments, when things got rough and the borrowers lost their jobs, they couldn't pay and stopped. Many of their mortgages went into foreclosure.

What finally happened, apparently, is that one day, a secretary for one of the secondary lenders was going through paperwork and happened to notice that a lot of foreclosures in the area involved borrowers who had originally purchased homes through Jim. An investigation was quietly launched. It was a simple matter to go back several years and check on the verifications of deposit with banks and S&Ls and the verifications of employment with employers. It quickly became clear that outright fraud had been committed.

As a result, Jim had his real estate business shut down. Even worse, the buyers were likewise charged with fraud. That meant that they were personally subject to any losses that the lenders incurred in the foreclosures as well as subject to civil and criminal penalties!

The moral of this story is that even a bad apple once in a great while can appear to be a shiny, bright one. Of course, as Barnum was heard to say, "You can never cheat an honest man." If those buyers had really thought it through, they would never have allowed Jim to falsify their verifications.

Picking the right agent is certainly the second most important decision you'll make—after picking the right house. Take the time to make it wisely.

7

Find the Right House in the Right Area at the Right Price

Once you've determined how much of a house you can afford (see Chapter 1), you can start the hunt. You'll want to marshal all the resources at your command to locate the perfect house.

However, simply darting about here and there won't do it. You have to set certain parameters. These usually include the following:

Set Your House-Hunting Parameters

How many bedrooms will you need? Most houses have three or four bedrooms. You'll probably have to pay a premium for five or more bedrooms. Houses with fewer than three bedrooms are often more difficult to resell, although they may cost less initially.

How many bathrooms will you need? Don't buy a house with only one bathroom. It's very difficult to resell.

Do you want a newer house with all the modern goodies such as better insulation, copper plumbing, high-efficiency heating and cooling, heavy-duty electrical systems, and what comes with all that—fewer repairs? Or will you settle for the comforts of an older, established home such as a fully grown garden, larger lot, and developed neighborhood? Do you want something new?

Are there any special features that you must have? (These include breakfast nooks, work area in the garage, washer and dryer near the bedroom, home office room(s), skylights, and wood paneling.) Try to be as flexible as possible. The more you must have, the more it's going to cost you.

Is there a better school district you want to be in? The better the neighborhood, almost invariably the better the schools. The two go together hand in hand.

What about being close to shopping? Most people don't want to drive more than a few minutes for bread or milk. Even if you're willing, will the next buyer be?

If you're going to commute, what is the maximum distance you are willing to drive? Get a map. Indicate those areas that are within range, those that are too far out. It will help you limit your search area.

Do you want a two-story, three-story, split-level, or ranch? Or will you accept any style?

What about colors? If you can't stand a blue house or a green house or a yellow house, you better recognize this fact up front. Are you willing to repaint?

Do you want a fireplace? What about a pool? Air conditioning? You'll pay substantially more for a pool house. However, a fireplace and even air conditioning (in many areas) are standard equipment these days. Expect to pay less for a house without them.

Do you want a big lot? Does it have to have a view? Do you mind being on a busy street? What about a corner lot? Big lots are supposed to be better and cost more. But in reality they require much more time, effort, and money to maintain and frequently are harder to resell. A lot with a view will always cost more, but it will bring more on resale. A corner lot means street noise on two sides and is often objectionable. Being on a busy street makes a house almost twice as hard to resell as being on a quiet street.

House-hunting Checklist

How many bedrooms do you need?_____

How many bathrooms?_____

New or old house?_____

School district to be in?_____

Close to shopping?_____
Close to transportation?_____
How many stories?_____
What colors?_____
Fireplace(s)?_____
Pool?_____
Spa?_____
Lot size?_____

Okay, let's say that you have an idea of what you want and you're ready to look. Where do you begin?

Start by checking the resources you have for finding just the right house. In most cases they include: checking the paper, driving around looking for "For Sale" signs, talking and working with agents, checking bulletin boards, talking to friends, acquaintances, and people at work and, of course, searching on the Internet (most listed homes are on the Internet either at *www.realtor.com* or some other Web site).

TIP—YOU MAKE YOUR PROFIT WHEN YOU BUY

People who buy a home to please themselves often have a harder time reselling later on. People who buy a home that is most likely to please others have an easier time reselling and selling for more money. When you buy, do so with an eye toward later reselling.

The important thing here is not to reinvent the wheel. When you begin looking for just the right house, what you're really doing is gathering information. You want to learn which neighborhoods you can afford and in which you feel safe, what those neighborhoods look like, what the traffic and public transportation are like, the quality of schools and shopping, and so forth.

It's a lot of information, and you want to get it the quickest and easiest way possible. One way is to go around investigating by yourself. In a few weeks you'll turn up most of the answers.

TIP—WHAT'S YOUR HOME OWNERSHIP HORIZON?

Most people plan on owning their next home forever. However, statistics suggest that the average length of ownership is only around 8 or 9 years. If you plan on reselling sooner, you may be willing to accept a less-than-perfect home choice. You should also look for a home that will resell more easily.

Another way is to check on the Internet. Information on schools, crime statistics, pricing, and more are available from many Web sites. Check out Online Resources at the end of this book.

Yet another method is to contact one or two good agents. Their business requires gathering this information. They already have it. In the matter of a single conversation, they can impart to you information it would take you days or sometimes weeks to gather on your own. They can also be an excellent source for directing you to others who may have knowledge that they don't possess.

TIP—KNOW WHERE YOU ARE

Always, always carry a map with you. When a broker says that the Maple Heights and Laurel Park areas are affordable, ask for the price range of those areas and then mark it on your map. You'll be surprised how 10 minutes later you can't remember whether it was Maple Park or Laurel Heights or whatever. When an agent tells you about schools or malls or public transportation, mark them on the map. Unless you're very familiar with the area, the information will be in one ear and out the other in moments.

How Do I "Sniff" Out the Areas?

Once you've whittled down the general areas that are in your price range, do some investigation on your own.

First, drive the areas. You should look for how people keep up their properties. Are all the lawns nicely mowed? Or are there broken cars and auto parts strewn across lawns? Watch for broken fences, scattered trash, and graffiti—sure signs the neighborhood is going downhill and may be unsafe.

Check the public transportation. Stop at the bus or train station and talk to people. Find out how long it really takes to commute.

Choosing a Good Neighborhood

- Good schools—Check test scores available at the district office.
- Low crime rate—Check with the police department's public affairs officer for crime statistics by neighborhood and block.
- Pride of ownership—Check to see that all the homes are well kept.
- Extras—Look for parks, wide streets, tall trees, cul-de-sacs, close to schools and shopping.
- Balance—Look for a mix of homes, apartments, condos, and townhouses. That produces diversity—a good place to live.
- Anchored—Look for a neighborhood that has few homes for sale and no detracting new influence (such as a commercial or industrial park coming in nearby).

If you're going to be driving on a thruway or freeway, wait until rush hour, then try it yourself. Use a watch to determine just how long it takes you. (You may be surprised!)

Check out public facilities. Look for libraries, fire stations, police departments, and hospitals as well as malls and grocery stores. Are they convenient and well located?

Walk the area. Once you've winnowed down the areas even more on the basis of items you discovered (above) by driving around, stop, park your car, and start walking. Talk to anyone you meet. Ask about problems in the area, about schools, about bad neighbors.

When you're doing this, you can also ask if people know of any house not yet listed that might be coming on the market soon. (We'll have more to say about this later.)

TRAP—GET OUT OF YOUR CAR

Don't be the sort of person who shops by car. Probably the biggest mistake that buyers make when checking out an area is not walking it. Nothing substitutes for shank's mare when it comes to discovering the kind of neighborhood you're in.

How Do I Find a Specific House?

By now you should have narrowed down the neighborhoods. You can afford and want to live between Ethel Street and Oak Boulevard or in the Pinewood or Horizon Hills or Wildfield tracts. You're ready to find the house. What you need to do is to quickly get a handle on every for-sale house in your price range in those areas.

Isn't that an overwhelming task?

Not really. Be aware that in most areas, 90 percent or more of the homes are listed with agents. The reason is simple: The vast majority of sellers don't have the time, expertise, or energy to sell their property themselves. (Also, it's a fact that buyers rarely purchase a home they "drop into" because of a "For Sale by Owner" sign. It's much easier to check with an agent who can produce a list.)

So start with the agents. Have an agent show you the listed houses in the area you're considering.

TIP—CHECK OUT THE "FSBOS"

You should check homes that are offered for sale by owner and are in the geographical area where you want to live. You might get lucky. See Chapter 13 for more info on how to do this.

Can I Find Properties Before They Are Listed?

There is another category of property that, though rarer, offers potentially greater financial opportunities to you, the buyer. This is a property that has not yet come onto the market.

Sellers have a world of reasons for selling. Sometimes it is a well-thought-out decision determined over a long period of time. In other cases a sudden event such as job change, illness, or death may cause a quick decision to sell.

Regardless of how it happens, there is always a period of time between when sellers make the decision (or are close to making the decision) and when they actually list the property with an agent. I call this the "golden time."

How Do I Find "Golden Time" Homes?

During the golden time, the sellers are willing to sell, but haven't yet fully committed to an agent or anyone else. If you can come in at that point with a reasonable offer, the sellers are very likely to accept. They will be thinking about all the hassles of selling that you will save them. No agents to deal with. No commission to pay. No time spent showing the property and waiting for buyers. You're a lifesaver if you come during that golden period.

Unfortunately, the golden time lasts only a few days to a few weeks. Also unfortunately, it's very hard to learn about sellers who are in that golden time. Often it's only through friends or acquaintances or associates at work that you learn that Jim is considering selling his home or Mary is planning to list her property.

When you do learn of this, however, act immediately. Contact Mary or Jim that very day or evening at the latest. Tell them you are actively looking to buy a home and would very much like to consider theirs. Will they just let you come over and look?

Then go look.

Chances are the house will be in a terrible location or will be too small or too big or too crazy. But every once in a while, it's just right. When it is, strike a deal right there and then.

Presumably by this time you know what houses are going for in the area and you know what a good price is. Come to terms and have your agent or attorney handle the paperwork later.

By getting to a house before it gets listed or goes up for sale, you can often save a lot of money and get superior terms. (Of course, you can hire an agent on a fee-for-service basis to handle all the paperwork.)

TIP—CONSIDER A FIXER

 You should also at least consider a fixer-upper, a home that is selling for less because it needs repair work. Sometimes you can find a sweet deal. Check Chapter 10 for details on how to find these.

Beware of Overbuilt Homes

You're looking at a house in a neighborhood that typically has three- and four-bedroom, single-story homes. Suddenly you come across a house with two stories and six bedrooms. The owner has "added on." There's an extra bath, a remodeled kitchen. In fact, the house looks like a palace. And the price is palatial.

Nevertheless, it offers so much that you're thinking of some way that you can get into it. Sell the car, the boat, the dog? Work an extra two jobs? Anything to get this wonderful house.

Forget it. The house is a loser, a white elephant. The only reason it looks so terrific is that it's a BMW surrounded by Fords. Put it with BMWs and Mercedes and Rolls Royces, and it'll look common.

There are a relatively few things that an owner can do to add on to a house and still recoup the money invested. Remodeling a kitchen is one. But start adding floors and rooms and very quickly the house becomes overbuilt—the neighborhood doesn't justify the work that's done.

Typically in such a situation, the owners are asking far less than the actual costs of the remodeling that they spent, but far more than surrounding houses cost. It's going to take them a very long time to find a buyer. And if you're that buyer, it's going to take you a very long time when you want to resell.

Buyers (like you) look for location first, the building second. If a house is too big or overbuilt for a location, it becomes a problem. You don't want to purchase someone else's problem.

TIP—BUY A LESS EXPENSIVE HOUSE, THE BEST NEIGHBORHOOD

Buy a less expensive house in the most expensive neighborhood you can afford. If you do, you multiply your chances for making money later on when you resell.

Don't Give Up

As you go from house to house, remember that a big factor is exhaustion. It's not just being physically tired. It's the fact that after a while, all the houses start to look the same. Therefore it's a good idea to keep in mind the following:

How to Avoid Buyer's Burnout

Always take a notepad and map with you. Mark the location of the house on the map and write down special features on the pad. If the owner offers you a fact sheet, save it even if you don't seem interested in the house at the time. Later on, you may think about it and realize the home had more appeal than you at first realized.

Never look at more than three or four houses in any one session. After that, you're no longer being careful. You're just running through, not paying attention to the details that could make you fall in love with a place. If you need to see a lot of houses, take big breaks. See three in the morning, then stop and have lunch. See three more, then stop and do something else. See three more in the early evening. Nine houses in one day is the absolute capacity of almost any prospective buyer. Even with nine, the features of one will begin to blend in with the features of another.

Try to get a Polaroid or digital camera and snap a picture of the houses that appeal to you. A picture *is* worth 1000 words. You'll instantly remember the features of a house, once you see a picture of the outside or some room inside. Frequently, agents or owners will provide you with photocopied pictures.

Sketch floor plans that you like on your notepad. It helps to remember and is also a good means of comparing one house with another.

Don't be afraid to ask questions. Many buyers worry that they'll be thought foolish if they ask about drainpipes or washrooms or taxes or something they think everyone else knows about. There are no foolish questions, only foolish buyers who don't ask questions. A seemingly simple question may open up a whole line of concern that you weren't aware of.

TIP—ASK, ASK, ASK!

 It's far better to ask about the problems of a house before you buy than to be stuck with them after you own it.

How Do I Know What the House is Worth? Get a CMA

Market value in real estate is determined by comparing what's for sale with what's sold. If a house in a tract sold for $250,000 a month ago and the nearly identical house next door is now for sale, it's a pretty good guess that it, too, is worth at least $250,000.

Once you find a house you are interested in, ask to see a CMA or "Comparable Market Analysis." Any good real estate agent can very quickly prepare a list of all the similar homes that have sold over the past six months to a year.

Check them out. Subtract for features your subject house lacks. Add for extras that your subject house has. For example, if the house that sold for $250,000 didn't have a pool and the house you are interested in does, add value for the pool. (Pools add to the price, but not much—it may cost $50,000 to put a pool in, but it may only add $10,000 to the home's price at sale time.) To learn how much the pool adds to your subject home, try to find other sales of similar homes with pools.

Traps of CMAs (Comparative Market Analyses)

- No two homes are ever exactly the same (add or subtract for floor plan, additions, size).
- No two lots (sites) are ever located exactly the same (add or subtract for view, size, quiet location).

- No two homes are ever in exactly the same condition (add or subtract for wear and tear, renovation, upkeep).

You can also find comparables online. Many Web sites, usually for a small fee, can give you comparables in most neighborhoods. It's a quick and easy way to get good information. See Online Resources at the end of this book.

8

Negotiate and Get a
Better Deal

Everyone's heard that the most important thing when buying a home is paying attention to location. While location certainly is important in getting a good deal, even more so is the ability to negotiate. In this chapter we're going to consider, "Negotiate, Negotiate, Negotiate!"

TIP—EVERYTHING IN REAL
ESTATE IS NEGOTIABLE!

Everything is negotiable when buying a house. The trouble is that most buyers either don't believe it or don't like to do it.

What's Negotiable When You
Buy a Home

Here's a *partial* list of what's negotiable when you buy a house:

- Price
- Financing
- Closing costs (except where specified by law)
- Occupancy (when you get the key and can move in)
- Painting (will the seller repaint a portion of or the entire house?)
- Repairs (will the seller repair the roof, plumb g, windows, and so on, and what kind and quality of repairs will be made?)

- Yard (will the seller remove unwanted trees or bushes, or put in desired landscaping?)
- Fixtures (which lights, fans, and appliances stay and which go?)
- Wall coverings (do the drapes stay or go?)
- Doghouse (does it go or stay?)
- Dog or cat (does it stay?)
- Furniture (will the seller throw in certain pieces?)
- Closing costs (will the seller pay yours?)
- And *everything else!*

Everything, with only rare exceptions, is up for grabs when you buy a home. How much you grab for yourself and how much the seller grabs depends on how well you negotiate. Of course, that's the rub. Many of us feel at a loss as negotiators.

For many people, in the back of their minds, they know they're going to come out second best. So they just don't bother. That's the trap.

That's a shame because negotiation gives the buyer incredible power in making a favorable transaction. Of course, it can also place him or her in a position of immense weakness. The fact is that how you negotiate determines whether you get the home of your dreams—or whether those dreams end up being a nightmare.

Do You Negotiate from Weakness?

I once had a friend who had a strong dislike for traveling in Mexico, even though her business obligations required that she routinely go to such places. "Why?" I asked her on one occasion. "The people are very friendly. The scenery in many areas is spectacular. And the currency exchange rate for Americans is often favorable. So what don't you like about it?" She glowered at me for a moment, then replied, "In many areas, particularly rural ones, you seldom know what the price of anything is." She waited for that to sink in, then continued, "You want to buy a pair of shoes. The price written on them is one thing. But you just know you should be able to get them for less, maybe half of that price if you haggle.

"But the moment you try to bargain, the seller gets upset and starts protesting, sometimes even accusing you of trying to steal food from the mouths of his children.

"He says you're trying to cheat him and demands the full price. I get embarrassed. I end up paying full price, sometimes even more just to get away! Why don't they just put the real price out there to begin with?"

I nodded understandingly and said, "But don't you see? The negotiation for the price is a kind of ritual. It's anticipated that you'll offer less and pay less than the asking price. The seller's insults and threats are just a way of doing business, trying to get you to pay more. *There's nothing personal in it.* Most people enjoy the negotiation."

She shook her head, then said, "I guess I'm just no good at negotiating."

I indicated that when I'd once visited Mexico, in a marketplace I'd seen a buyer and seller haggle for nearly half an hour over the price of some small trinket, hurling accusations of thievery and insults relating to family origin. All the hostility was immediately forgotten the moment the sale was concluded, at which time both buyer and seller embraced each other as though they were bosom buddies. "Negotiation for price and even terms of sale is the accepted practice throughout most of the world. It is an ancient and honored tradition."

My friend scowled at me. "It's not a tradition in the United States. When I go into a department store, I know what the price is. There are no shenanigans, no arguing, no negotiations. If a pair of shoes in Macy's is listed at $65, that's the price—no ifs, ands, or buts!"

I nodded and thought about the last time I was in Macy's and bought a sweater. The full market price was $60. But, it was half off because of a sale. And because I was there early on a Saturday I could take another 25 percent off. And if I opened a credit card, it was another 10 percent off . . .

It was the end of our conversation. My friend was absolutely convinced that negotiating was the bane of doing business.

How wrong she was.

Negotiation is alive and well everywhere, including in the United States. No, you won't likely recognize it openly when you go to most stores, although it is reflected in sales and cut-rate prices. On the other hand, it is most clearly seen when you buy high-ticket items, like a car, or rare coins or paintings, or . . . real estate. Negotiation for price or terms of sale always has been and probably always will be the *rule* in any capitalist society. It's how true market price is discovered.

How Do I Negotiate in Real Estate?

Which brings us back to buying a home. Here, everything is negotiable—the most important items usually being the price and the terms. If you're a good negotiator, you may end up paying 5 to 30 percent or more below what the seller is asking. Negotiation is an inherent part of buying real estate and if you're going to participate, you should plan on learning the basic skills.

Should I Rely on the Agent?

At this point, I'm sure some readers are saying, "Hold on. I worked with an agent when I bought my last home. The agent did my negotiating. The agent saw that I got a good price."

I doubt it. You may have gotten a good price, but if you did, it was largely because of your own efforts. The agent in many cases is the *seller's* agent, with a fiduciary responsibility to the seller to find a buyer. In most states it is unethical if not outright illegal for the seller's agent to even suggest that you offer less than the seller is asking!

This doesn't mean that agents don't, in fact, do so. In my experience many agents do. But they may couch their suggestions in language such as, "The sellers have indicated that they are anxious to sell and that they'd be agreeable to an offer of a little less than the asking price." Indeed. The sellers may be desperate and may be willing to take an offer of 25 percent less than the asking price. But the agent can't come right out and tell you that if he or she represents the seller, unless they have authorized her to say it.

In addition, most agents don't really want you to make a lowball offer. The lower your offer, the harder it is for the agent to get the seller to accept, and the less chance there is of getting a commission. (The agent normally gets a commission only when there's a sale.) On the other hand, if you offer just a *little bit less,* sure the seller might be willing to accept that. A sale is quickly made and a commission obtained.

So instead of offering $25,000 less than the asking price, you offer $5000 less—and get it. The seller is happy. The agent's happy.

And you, you big dummy, are happy because you think you got yourself a "good price."

The point is that you can't rely on anyone but yourself when it comes to negotiation. A good agent can handle the actual mechanics of speaking for you to the seller, and that's certainly a big plus. But the agent can't or at least shouldn't tell you what to offer.

It's ultimately up to you to determine what the parameters of the negotiation are going to be. You set the price, the terms, and all the other conditions of sale that you will accept. (Also see Chapter 6 for picking a good *buyer's* agent.)

Are You Your Own Worst Enemy?

Which brings us back to you. Most house hunters, particularly house hunters who don't regularly invest in real estate, are worried about hurting the seller's feelings, about insulting the agent by offering a price far lower than the asking price, and most important, about doing anything that would appear foolish.

If that's the way you feel when you open negotiations for the purchase of your next home, you are a gone goose. Remember the example of buying shoes in Mexico? The seller and buyer in Mexico often argue back and forth for a long time, haggling over the price. But then, when it's all said and done, they shake hands and become bosom buddies.

Well, you may not end up bosom buddies with the seller, but remember that when negotiating for real estate you are participating in that same age-old ritual of bargaining. You are relying on your own cleverness and personal will power.

If you are weak and susceptible to the influence of the seller (or the seller's agent), you could be talked into paying a higher price, getting less favorable terms, or (worst of all) accepting a house that you really don't want. On the other hand, if you are a good "horse trader" you are going to get a good deal all around.

Can I Negotiate on a New House?

A few exceptions are in order here. Sometimes you're buying a brand new home instead of a resale. The builder/developer has a set price written in ink on the brochure. Either you pay that price, you are told, or you don't get the home. Right?

It depends. If the market is hot and new homes are selling as fast as they can be put up, yes, you'll have to pay the set price. In fact, when the market is very hot people will sometimes camp out in front of builder/developers' offices for days just for the privilege of paying full price for a new home!

On the other hand, if the market is slow, there's no reason you can't offer a builder/developer a lower price—and get it. (Just remember that builder/developers often have a relatively small profit margin and they may not be able to accept a severely reduced price. See Chapter 12 on buying a brand new home from a builder/developer.)

Should I Negotiate Directly with the Seller?

Sometimes sellers will bypass the use of an agent and attempt to sell their homes themselves. (In the trade these are called FSBOs—for sale by owners.) The temptation is to think that because no agent is involved, the seller doesn't have to pay a commission and, hence, can offer a lower price.

Maybe. On the other hand, you now not only have to set the parameters of your negotiations (price and terms) but also you have to carry those negotiations out face to face.

If you're a good horse trader and if the seller is too, things should go fine and no agent may be needed. But, unfortunately, in our country most people have been inured into thinking in terms of fixed prices and not negotiation. Hence, when you offer the seller far less than he or she is asking, you could be asked to leave in not so pleasant terms and further negotiations may be impossible.

Or, if the seller is a good negotiator and you aren't, when your low offer is rejected along with suggestions that you've insulted the seller's integrity, you may be put off and leave without realizing that it was all part of the game.

As a result, for the vast majority of people, buying direct from sellers (contrary to what the TV "get rich quick" gurus of real estate may push) is more difficult, and less likely to result in a good price and terms, than dealing with a broker/agent. (I'll have a lot more to say about working directly with a seller in Chapter 13.)

Can I Learn to Negotiate Successfully?

In the old days in real estate (by old days I mean as late as the 1950s) the Latin expression "caveat emptor" was often quoted: "Let the buyer beware." Since that time, consumer protection laws have swelled to the point where today the buyer who knows how to take advantage of these laws is protected and even has advantages as never before.

However, when it comes to the actual negotiations, there are no protections for the buyer. You are at your own mercy. You can make a good deal. Or you can get yourself into terrible trouble.

The question naturally arises, therefore, of how a person who is not a real estate professional can negotiate successfully in what may be a den of wolves. How do you avoid cheating yourself by your negotiation inexperience?

The answer is by acquiring knowledge. Having read this chapter thus far, you've already acquired a great deal that you may not have known before. You now know that everything is negotiable. When the agent says, "There's no way you can ask for the refrigerator. It's personal property and goes with the seller automatically." You can stand back, catch your breath, and say with confidence, "Either I get that damn refrigerator or there's no deal!" Grumbling, the agent will write into the contract that the refrigerator goes with the house, knowing full well that he or she is going to have to fight the sellers for hours to get them to agree.

You should now know that there's nothing embarrassing about submitting low offers and making your agent struggle to get the seller to sign. There's nothing wrong with insisting on terms that are totally favorable to you. You should also now know that it's a mistake to let the seller's agent "assist" you in determining the price to offer.

Finally, you should now know that there's nothing foolish about getting down on the ground and scrambling for price and terms.

It's an ancient tradition that, regardless of your particular background, is your human heritage. You were born to do it!

Knowledge Is Power

The best way to negotiate is to negotiate from strength. There is only one way to get strength: through knowledge.

Ultimately, how you fare when buying a home is going to be a direct result of the knowledge you have. The more you know about the condition of the house, the motivation of the seller, and the state of the market, the better a position you'll be in to negotiate from strength.

How do you get that knowledge? In the next chapters we'll go over much of what you need to know. We'll look at common and not-so-common traps that most buyers fall into. Hopefully, perhaps for the first time in your house-hunting experience, you will have the tools in hand to become a good negotiator.

Once you know how the game works, you can play. Now, here are some quick tips for negotiating that you may find particularly helpful:

Tips for Negotiating

- Never be insulting—remember, it's only business. If you insult an agent or seller, you can turn it into a personal fight, which you'll probably lose.

- Get time on your side—Give the sellers very little time to make a decision on your offer, perhaps 12–24 hours or less. It forces them to choose and helps prevent a better offer from slipping in.

- Appear "hard nosed"—If you convince your agent you won't pay any more, he or she will more likely be able to convince the seller.

- Find out the seller's motivation—If the seller is out of work, has been transferred, the house must be sold in a divorce, or the seller otherwise must move quickly, consider a lowball offer. A desperate seller should be willing to give you a better deal.

- Be willing to compromise (counteroffer)—but only when you're absolutely sure you can't get your original offer.

■ If you can't get your price, try to get your terms—sellers are often hung up on price. If you give them their price, they may be willing to give you a low-interest rate mortgage, lots of personal property, early possession, or almost anything else that you might need, which may be worth more than price to you.

For more information on the topic of this chapter, you may also want to read, *Tips and Traps When Negotiating Real Estate*—Irwin, (McGraw-Hill, 1995).

9

How to Lowball Sellers and Get Your Offer Accepted

I've never heard of a buyer who boasted about paying too much for a home. We all want to get the lowest price we can, a price that we feel makes the property a good value at the least, a bargain at best.

But how do we achieve that?

If you ask your agent, you may meet resistance. Most agents would prefer an easy negotiation, which means that you come in at close to full value. (Remember, an agent doesn't normally get paid unless there's a sale.) In addition, the agent may be working for the seller (unless you're using a dual or buyer's agent) and may not owe you allegiance.

Consequently, in many ways when you ask your real estate agent how much to offer, you're in a position similar to asking an automobile salesperson how much to offer. You're asking the wrong person. You're, in effect, asking the seller, or at the least, someone who's more interested in getting any deal, rather than a good deal for you.

Whom should you ask?

Rely on Yourself

If you've been looking at homes for a while, you should have a pretty good idea what similar houses are listed for. This gives you a good idea of the price range your prospective house is in.

TIP—HOMES RARELY SELL FOR
LISTED PRICE

 Selling prices and listing prices are usually different. In most markets they sell for less than listed. In some hot markets, of course, they may actually sell for more!

Check the "comps." Ask your agent to let you see the selling prices of similar homes going back at least a year. Any agent worth her salt has these figures readily available from a listing service—see Chapter 7. (You can also sometimes get this info from the Internet—see Internet Resources at the end of this book.)

Pick out all sales for similar houses, then try to get as close a match as possible (same number of bedrooms, bathrooms, pool, amenities). In an active market you'll find half a dozen sales or more.

Extra features such as a new kitchen or bathroom or other remodeling do add to the value of a house. However, they don't normally make the house significantly more valuable than its neighbors. Any house that's priced more than 5 percent above its neighbors because of improvements may be a "white elephant."

Also, it's important not to feel sorry for sellers who have sunk a ton of money into remodeling and are now trying to get every penny back from you. It's not up to you to bail them out of their foolishness. Remember to recheck the comps. See if you can find a home that recently sold that also had similar improvements, and compare prices.

How Much Should I Offer?

Sellers in most markets ask more that they are willing to take for their homes. They are expecting to come down some, hence the above-market asking price. If you pay what the seller is asking, you could be wasting money. The real trick is knowing how much less than asking price a seller will take.

Sometimes a seller will only come down a few thousand dollars. Other times they may drop 10 percent or more. And, of course, there's that occasional seller who refuses to come down a dime. (And in very hot markets, there are multiple offers from buyers, and to win you must pay more than asking price!)

Unless you've got supernatural powers (or the seller's agent spills the beans), you don't know. That means you have to learn through the negotiating process. Your offer and each counter-offer the sellers make tells you more. Eventually, if you're a good negotiator, you will have gotten the lowest possible price.

Should I Lowball the Seller?

It all starts out with a low bid. You can't very well go lower after you've previously made a high bid; you would lose credibility and the seller's interest.

However, if you bid too low initially, the seller may not believe that you're in earnest in buying the property and may simply turn your offer down without even a counter. Which brings up the biggest risk when lowballing, you may lose the property entirely.

Now it's a matter of understanding yourself. From an investment perspective, it's better to lowball 10 houses and not get any of them than to pay too much for one house.

On the other hand, if you're looking at this property more as a home than as an investment, you may not want to risk losing it. You may feel that you'll simply die if you don't get it. You just *can't* lose it!

If that's the way you feel, then don't bother with lowball offers. They're simply too risky for you. Come in close to full price, so that this one won't get away. (In a very hot market, you may want to offer full or even more than full price!)

TRAP—KNOW THYSELF

Are you more investor or more habitat buyer? Are you in love with the property? Or can you just walk away? Are you willing to make offers on a dozen properties before getting one? Or is the whole process so overwhelming that you simply want to get it over with? How you answer these questions should guide how low . . . or high an offer you make.

How Much Should I Lowball?

You may want to offer as much as 25 percent or more less than the asking price. However, that's usually just a test offer, trying to see what the water's like. In all but a very cold market, a seller's likely to simply reject it out of hand. Indeed, the seller may simply ignore the offer and not counter it, and that could mean the end of the deal for you. Often the goal of the initial lowball is to get a counter-offer from the seller. Try to offer enough to entice the seller to at least respond.

The counter-offer can be very revealing. If it's just a thousand dollars or so off the asking price (or right at the asking price), you can assume that this seller won't budge much. Then it's time to fish or cut bait. Either move up to the seller's price, or move on.

Remember, to succeed with making lowball offers you must be willing to make a lot of them. You have to play the odds. You have to expect that most of the time they will simply be ignored.

What If the Seller Counteroffers?

It's a good sign. It's a better sign if the seller accepts your original offer. But a counter means the seller is willing to dicker with you. After a seller counters at a significantly lower price (but not as low as you've originally offered), you've really got only three alternatives:

1. Accept the seller's counter, if you think it's low enough.

2. Counter at a price compromising halfway between your original offer and the seller's first counter-offer. (You can't both accept and counter. Countering is making a new offer.)

3. Repeat your original offer, if you think it's a good price.

Compromising at halfway between the seller's last offer and your original offer (#2 above), may land the deal. Or the seller may cut the remaining distance in half again with yet another counter. Or again the seller may simply pick up his or her marbles and leave the game. If the seller does counter, however, you're well along toward getting the home at a reasonable price.

Sticking to your original offer (reoffering it as your first counter) has some negotiating drawbacks. It tells the seller to take it or leave it. It says you're not willing to compromise.

A certain percentage of the time (no one knows how much, but it's not high), you'll win by holding pat. The seller will indeed capitulate and accept your original offer. This usually only happens, however, in a cold market and with a desperate seller.

More likely the seller will simply throw up his or her hands and say there's no dealing with you. The seller will then simply walk away. After all, if you don't raise your offer, what choice have you left the seller but to take your offer, or quit?

My suggestion is that unless you think your original lowball offer is actually realistic, always counter the seller's counter, even if you only come up a thousand dollars or so. It keeps the negotiations open and gives the seller another chance to come down even more!

Eventually, you'll get the house you want at the price you want to pay. Or you'll move on.

TIP—GET AN AGENT WHO WANTS TO MAKE YOUR OFFER

Some agents simply refuse to take a "lowball" offer. They may say something like, "I can't take this offer to the seller. You'll just have to offer more." Baloney. The seller's agent has to take every legitimate offer to the seller. A legitimate offer is one that is in writing with a deposit. Your agent may not like it, but he or she will do it. On the other hand, if the agent is reticent to submit the offer, you'd do better by finding a different agent who is more willing to try to get your price accepted.

By the way, if you are using a buyer's agent (as described in the Chapter 6), it is incumbent on that agent to get for you the best price the seller is likely to accept. You can rely much more heavily on a buyer's agent's advice than on a seller's agent's or a dual agent's comments.

Have You Asked the Sellers What's Their Lowest Price?

This may come as a surprise to many buyers. "You mean I can talk to the seller?" Of course you can. The worst the seller can say is, "I'm not discussing the sale. Talk to my agent." The best the seller can do is to tell you how desperate he or she is and how urgently a sale is needed—and how low an offer might be accepted.

TRAP—AGENTS DON'T LIKE
PRINCIPALS TALKING TOGETHER

 Your agent isn't likely to encourage you to talk to the seller. That bypasses the agent and arouses all kinds of suspicions (like maybe you're trying to finagle a deal to avoid paying a commission). Don't worry. They won't put you behind bars for talking to the seller. Just remember, the seller is only a phone call away.

On the other hand, don't try to bypass the agent to avoid the commission—even though a seller may suggest this, offering to split the cost of the commission through a lower price. You probably won't succeed and you'll only offend the agent, who you want to be on your side.

If an agent shows you the property, then almost certainly the house is tied up by an exclusive listing. The only way for the seller to avoid paying a commission is to wait until the listing has expired.

Even then, most listing agreements provide that a commission must be paid to an agent for months after the listing expires if the buyer (you) was shown the house during the listing period by the agent.

You would have to wait months in order for this finagling to be effective, and during that time chances are that someone else would come along and buy the property out from under you.

Have You Tried Hiring an Appraiser?

The trouble with hiring an appraiser is that it usually takes too much time and is too expensive (typically $150 to $300). But if you have the time and want a professionally acquired figure for the true market value of the property, you can call in an appraiser. And if the appraisal comes in low, it can provide ammunition to blast the seller down from a high asking price.

Appraisers usually work on a fee basis for lenders.

Chances are that if you're going to get a mortgage on the property, you'll need an appraisal anyway. This way, you'll just get it sooner.

However, not all appraisers are approved by every lender. If you intend to save money on an appraisal by using it for both setting the price and obtaining a mortgage, be sure you know in advance which appraiser your lender uses. Also, cut a deal with the appraiser so you don't get charged twice. Finally, remember that even if you ultimately don't purchase the property, you're still liable for the cost of the appraisal.

Appraisers can be recommended by lenders. They are also listed in the yellow pages of your phone directory. Those who have MAI (American Institute of Real Estate Appraisers) or SREA (Society of Real Estate Appraisers) designations are members of professional appraisal organizations and have usually completed extensive courses in appraising.

Have You Tried an Appraisal Offer?

A daring approach is to make an offer with the price contingent upon an appraisal. In other words, you'll agree to accept whatever the appraiser says the property is worth if the seller will likewise accept it. (Usually there are "outs" included, which provide that if the price is above a certain point, you won't accept or if it's below a certain point, the seller doesn't have to go through with it.)

An offer contingent on appraisal (described above) is sometimes done with investment properties, but rarely with houses. Nevertheless, if you have a seller who's convinced that the sales price is right and won't budge, it's another alternative. Just be sure that you agree in advance on who the appraiser is and who is to pay the appraisal fee.

10

What You Should Worry About in the Purchase Agreement

The whole process of buying a home is defined by the purchase agreement (also sometimes called the "sales offer" or "deposit receipt"). It's the governing document of the transaction. Once your offer is accepted, it becomes what ultimately determines how the rest of the sale is handled, what you get, for how much money, and on what terms.

How We Got to Today's Purchase Agreements

In the old days in real estate, the sales agreement was usually just one page long. It had very little printed material and was composed mostly of empty spaces that the agent filled out. That has changed dramatically.

Over the years dissatisfied buyers and sellers (a small minority, but with important implications) have gone to court, fighting over various issues such as contingencies, deposits, and damages. What they discovered was that the sales agreement, drawn up not by an attorney but by a real estate agent, might not hold up. In fact, in some cases the agreement was downright defective.

This resulted in additional suits, sometimes against agents, almost all of whom now carry a form of malpractice or errors and omissions insurance.

103

It also resulted in a new kind of sales agreement. The new agreement is usually created by attorneys and is frequently many pages long. Almost all of it is printed out—the agent typically only checks boxes or fills in dollar amounts.

In fact, there are very few places where the agent (or you) even have the opportunity to write anything new. The whole emphasis is on seeing to it that relatively little can be added or changed for fear that it may void or weaken the agreement.

TIP—HAVE YOUR ATTORNEY CHECK IT OUT

 Because the sales agreement is intended to be a legally binding document, you should have your real estate attorney check it over and explain the full ramifications of it to you before you sign it.

In addition to legal considerations, which you should pursue with your attorney, there are important practical issues in the purchase agreement that involve the kind of a deal you're going to get. These typically include the following areas: (If yours does not cover these areas, you should ask your agent or attorney why it does not?)

Practical Areas Your Purchase Agreement Should Cover

- Price, down payment, and deposit
- Specific terms for all financing
- Street improvements or bonds (if any, who pays for them)
- When you will be given occupancy?
- How long does the seller have to accept the offer?
- The term of the escrow (how long it will be open)
- How you will take title (tenants in common, joint tenancy, community property, and so on; see your lawyer, since there are important tax and legal ramifications for how you take title)
- Liquidated damages and arbitration in case of disputes
- Any personal property involved

- Foreign tax withholding (applies if the seller is a foreigner)
- When and how the sellers will give you a disclosure statement about the property
- Seller's warranties
- When and how you'll be able to conduct a professional inspection
- When and how a termite report will be issued
- If soil or geological tests (found in areas with earthquakes or other soil problems) will be conducted)
- If there are concerns about flood or water hazards (noting if the property is in any flood hazard area)
- Other disclosures, such as zoning problems (indicating if the property is in a special zone, such as a "coastal zone," which could affect your ability to build or add on)
- If you get a Home Protection Plan (which pays for damage or problems with the heating, plumbing, electrical, and other systems, and who pays for it)
- Energy retrofit disclosure procedures (local or state ordinances, for example, sometimes require additional insulation to be placed in the house when the property is sold)
- How pro rations will be handled
- Other contingencies involved in the sale

Many of the areas covered by the sales agreement, such as price, are obvious. Others are discussed in different sections of this book. Below, however, we're going to look at some selected areas of a typical sales agreement that usually are of particular interest to buyers.

How Big a Deposit Should I Give?

Once you've settled on the price, the next consideration for most buyers is the deposit. The deposit is money that you put up at the time you make an offer on a piece of property to show that you are in earnest about buying it. (You're putting your money where your mouth is, so to speak.) Hence the deposit is actually "earnest money." It is supposed to demonstrate to the seller that your offer isn't capricious.

An offer can be made without a deposit. However, a seller is less likely to accept it. After all, without a deposit you have very little to lose by not following through on the deal.

Some agents will insist that you put up a big deposit. They argue that this will help convince the seller to accept your offer. While there is a germ of truth here, there is also a lot of chaff, as we'll see shortly. You can offer any amount as a deposit.

TRAP—DON'T BE BULLIED INTO MAKING A BIG DEPOSIT

 Today, a good agent may suggest you simply put up $1000 to $10,000 "to make the offer official." Of course, that same agent may insist that you be willing to increase that offer substantially once all contingencies have been removed.

Agents often suggest that you offer 5 percent of the purchase price. On a $100,000 property that's $5000. But on a $500,000 property, it's $25,000.

To my thinking, in today's market any initial deposit of more than $5000, or $10,000 for a very expensive home, is a waste. You're simply putting your money unnecessarily at risk. The reason is that, unlike in the past, today's deals hinge on all sorts of contingencies. For example, the deal is rarely solid until you've approved a professional inspection report and the seller's disclosures. If these contingencies aren't removed, the deal doesn't go forward and your deposit is normally returned.

Thus, a large deposit today doesn't mean what it used to. It won't impress the seller's agent. And it won't impress a sharp seller. (They would be more impressed by a solid pre-approval letter from a lender.)

TIP—A DEPOSIT IS MONEY AT RISK

 No matter how likely it is that your deposit will be returned, any money you put up is at risk. Therefore, it's to your advantage to put as little at risk as possible.

Remember, you can agree to add to the deposit later, after you've removed the contingencies.

Sellers may demand in the purchase agreement that once the offer has been accepted and you've had a chance to inspect and approve the property and disclosures (and perhaps once financing has been arranged), you will put up an additional amount of money in the deposit. This could be a substantial increase.

Increasing the deposit has two important effects. It assures the seller that you are serious (in earnest) about completing the transaction. And second, it means that you might lose your deposit, since you've already cleared the contingencies that might otherwise allow you to gracefully get it back.

You won't want to increase your deposit unless and until you're sure you want to and are able to go through with the purchase. On the other hand, refusing to increase your deposit, as agreed to in the purchase offer, could nix the deal.

Must a Deposit Be in Cash?

A deposit doesn't necessarily have to be in the form of cash. It can be a promissory note or a check that all parties agree not to cash or even personal property such as the title to a car or boat. Cash (cashier's check), however, talks the loudest when you're trying to convince a seller to accept an offer.

Sometimes sellers will specify in a listing agreement that they will accept no offers with less than, for example, a $5000 cash deposit. Remember, however, everything is negotiable. You can always offer a smaller deposit in a different form.

However, if the seller is demanding a $5000 cash deposit, the agent may not be required to submit lesser offers, depending on how the listing agreement was signed.

Most agents, however, will submit any and all offers.

Will I Get My Deposit Back?

At this point, I'm sure some readers are wondering, "What's the big deal, anyway? Why not put up a bigger deposit?" Too often buyers simply assume that everything is bound to turn out okay. If the deal sours, they'll get their money back.

In most cases, this in fact is the way it does turn out. But not always. Sometimes when things go bad, they can go bad very quickly and very badly, particularly in terms of the deposit.

There are at least two problem areas you should know about: 1.) Who gets the deposit? 2.) How do you get it back if the deal falls through?

Who Holds the Deposit?

The seller is entitled to the deposit. However, the seller is the last person in the world you want to give the deposit to. The seller might immediately spend the money, then later on, if the deal falls through, might not be able to refund it to you, even if you're entitled to get it back. It could require the services of an attorney and a lawsuit to secure the return of the deposit from the seller, and that could be very costly. In other words, giving the deposit to the seller could be like dropping it down a deep hole.

You want the deposit to go to a neutral party who will not frivolously spend the money, but who will hold it and have it on hand to pay you back, if necessary. The first most likely candidate here is the agent.

Should I Give My Deposit to My Agent?

Real estate agents are required to maintain trust accounts for any money they receive. In other words, they can't commingle (mix) your money with their own, but must hold it in a separate account in trust for you. This is to keep them from spending your money. While that sounds safe, the problem is that, in theory, the deposit belongs to the seller and if the seller demands it, the seller's agent is supposed to hand the deposit over. Most agents, however, are as wary of the seller as you are and will do everything possible to hold the money in trust until the deal closes.

TIP—AGENTS MUST MAINTAIN FIDUCIARY ACCOUNTS

In many states the most common reason for real estate license suspension or revocation is the commingling (mixing) of the agent's funds with yours. It's not that

agents are all that dishonest; it's that they are sometimes lousy accountants.

To ensure that they don't lose their license, agents will almost
always bend over backwards to repay any money stuck in their trust
account. Further, many states have special recovery funds. If you lose
money through the carelessness (or fraud) of an agent, you may be
able to recover it from the state, even though it could take years.
Check with your state's department of real estate.

Should I Give My Deposit to an Escrow Company?

Today, many good agents realize that accepting a check for a
deposit puts them at great risk. If the deal doesn't go through,
both the buyer and the seller may demand the money, leaving the
agent in the middle. To avoid this, many agents suggest you write
the deposit check to an escrow company that you agree in
advance will handle the escrow of the property if and when the
seller accepts. In other words, give the deposit to a neutral party.
Sound good?

There is also peril here. If after the seller accepts, the deal still
falls apart, even through no fault of your own, it might be hard to
get the deposit back even from a neutral escrow.

The reason is that escrows simply handle the documents and
funds in a transaction. In order for an escrow to operate, both buyer
and seller must agree to the escrow's instructions. If, for example,
you tell the escrow to return your money and the seller tells the
escrow to hold onto it, there's no agreement. And your money
remains in limbo. This affects you more than the seller. After all, it's
your money.

Sometimes in this situation sellers are content to let the money
sit in an inactive escrow for months just to "punish" a buyer for
a deal that falls through. Fortunately, calmer minds usually prevail and sellers eventually will agree to release your funds, once
they become convinced that there's no way they can get the
money and that to continue to hold it might result in a lawsuit
against them.

TIP—CONSIDER GIVING THE DEPOSIT TO ESCROW

Making your check payable to an escrow does ensure that it goes to a neutral party. It does not, however, ensure that you'll get it back quickly, easily, or at all.

What If the Deal Falls Through?

What must be obvious by now is that putting up a deposit is sometimes a tricky thing that can have significant consequences. How do you get the deposit back, for example, if the deal doesn't go through?

There are at least two considerations here: First, why didn't the deal go through? If it's your fault, you may not be entitled to a return of the deposit. Second, if you are entitled to a return, how do you get the funds transferred back to you?

Operating on the principle that the time to consult an attorney is before you need one, I advise you to seek the services of a professional real estate lawyer at this juncture. Chances are you're going to need one anyway before the deal is concluded, and by bringing the lawyer in at an early stage, you could avoid much grief.

(Most lawyers who deal in real estate have set fees that are much lower than for general legal work. Ask the lawyer in advance what the fees are.)

What If the Seller Doesn't Accept My Offer?

That's easy, or should be. If the seller does not accept your offer, you're entitled to your deposit back, immediately. It's just that simple.

The seller has to agree to your entire offer, including any terms you propose. If the seller agrees to the price but not the terms and counters with different terms, which you don't accept, there's no deal and you're entitled to your money back. If the seller accepts your terms but counters with a different price, which you don't accept, the deal's off and you're entitled to your deposit back.

The moment the seller declines your offer and "counters" (proposes a deal different in some way, no matter how small), the original offer is dead. Unless you accept the seller's counteroffer, you're entitled to your deposit back.

Once in a very great while an unscrupulous agent will say something such as, "Even though the seller didn't accept, I made a good-faith effort to get the deal through. Therefore, I'm entitled to half the deposit. I'll return half to you and keep the other half."

No way. In the typical purchase offer, the agent gets a commission only if the deal is consummated. If the seller never agrees, no commission is due. Politely tell the agent you want your entire deposit back immediately or you will report the agent to the state department of real estate. That should do it. (Note: If you sign an agreement with a buyer's agent, be sure to read it carefully, especially with regard to how the deposit is handled.)

What If the Seller Accepts and Then, Later On, the Deal Falls Through Because of Me?

There are many reasons the deal might fall through because of your fault. For example, you could be counting on Aunt Harriet to give you the money for the down payment. You get the seller to sign an offer, secure financing, and poor Aunt Harriet has a heart attack and dies. Her money will be tied up in probate for years.

Sure, you didn't do anything intentionally to quash the deal, but you don't have the expected money to perform. As far as the seller is concerned, it's your fault.

Or you get cold feet. You take a look at those huge monthly payments and you decide that you can't go through with it. You want out, period.

Or you find another house that is really perfect. You want to get out of this deal so that you can get the other.

Or . . . There are lots of reasons that you might not want to or not be able to complete your end of a purchase agreement. The point here is, however, that for whatever reason, it's your fault the deal doesn't go forward, and if you don't have a contingency clause protecting you (see below), what are your chances of getting the deposit back?

Put simply, your chances are not good. In fact, you could be in hot water and liable for a lot more than just the deposit if the seller decides to sue you for specific performance (demanding that you complete the transaction).

Most sales agreements provide that if you default, the seller is entitled to keep the deposit. (Separately, the listing agreement between seller and agent may specify that they will split the deposit in the event of your default.) Thus, at least in theory, as soon as you default on the deal, your deposit is lost. And, of course, there could be an irate seller to deal with.

In the past when a buyer defaulted, a seller occasionally did sue for damages, thus tying up the courts and causing long-term problems for everyone concerned. As a result, liquidated-damage clauses for residential real estate have come into wide use in sales agreements and are accepted and even codified in many states.

Will a "Liquidated Damages" Clause Protect Me?

Basically these clauses state that if you and the seller agree in advance, the deposit (or a portion of it) will constitute the entire damages the seller is entitled to in the event of your default. In other words, if the deal doesn't go through and it's clearly your fault, you agree in advance that the seller can keep the deposit, provided she or he agrees not to sue you for additional damages or specific performance.

Many states put limitations on liquidated damages. In order to keep more, the seller has to prove in a court of law that it's reasonable to hang onto the money. If you want your money back, you have to prove that it's reasonable for you to get it. Either way, for practical purposes, the seller is usually satisfied and unless you're litigious by nature, you probably are satisfied, too. (Of course, both seller and buyer can agree to virtually any amount as liquidated damages, though it's normally not to your advantage as buyer to agree to a high amount.)

You may be asked to sign or initial a clause in the sales agreement that states that if you do not go through with the sale, your deposit is automatically forfeited in exchange for the seller not suing you for specific performance. Should you sign?

Ask your attorney. On the one hand, signing the clause (assuming the sellers also signs) helps to limit your loss to the deposit receipt. (It does not guarantee it—there are few guarantees in life!) On the other hand, it almost ensures that you'll lose the entire deposit, whereas, depending on the situation, you might otherwise get at least a portion back.

What If There Are Extenuating Circumstances?

While what potentially can or cannot happen may seem quite dire, what actually happens in practice can be somewhat different. If you simply back out because you change your mind or find a better house, chances are that neither the seller's agent nor the seller is going to be sympathetic, and you stand an excellent chance of having them demand your deposit.

However, if circumstances cause you to default—your aunt, whom you were counting on for money, dies or you get sick or injured or something happens that is truly beyond your control—then it's often a different story. Here, you are truly relying on the goodwill of the seller's agent and the seller. In most cases where I have seen this happen, the buyer has gotten most, if not all, of the deposit back.

Agents are not in the business to make money on deposits.

Sellers are interested in selling, not in keeping the deposit of a person who falls on hard times. I have seen agents bend over backward in these circumstances to get the seller to give the deposit back. I have seen sellers gladly return the deposit, sometimes over the agent's objections. Of course, you could get the bad apples, but goodwill in people is everywhere.

What If the Seller (Not You) Fails to Go Through with the Deal?

Why would a seller fail to go through with a deal, once signed?

Simple. You offer $150,000 for a house and the seller accepts. Two days later another buyer comes in with an offer of $175,000. Wouldn't it be wonderful if the seller could get out of your deal and accept the new one? The seller would stand to make an additional $25,000. That's plenty of reason to default.

In these circumstances you are fully justified in demanding the return of your deposit. In addition, you may want to sue the seller for specific performance, to force a sale to you. (After all, you could then resell for the higher price and keep the profit yourself!)

When the seller defaults, you usually will get the deposit back. Usually the seller is more than happy to do everything to get that deposit back to you in the hope that you won't take further action.

If you still want the property, check with your attorney. You may decide to take further action.

What If It's No One's Fault, but the Deal Just Can't Be Made?

There are a lot of reasons that a deal might not go through. You may not be able to secure adequate financing. The title to the property may not be clear. There could be extensive termite damage.

It could turn out that the house is in the middle of a flood plain. The reasons are endless, and they crop up in a good many deals.

In most cases there's a way to work them out. Other financing is secured. The seller clears the title. The termite damage is fixed. You agree to accept the risk of flood damage for a lower price, and so on. In other words, the problems are solved one way or another.

However, sometimes it just doesn't work and there's no deal to be made. What happens to your deposit then?

If you've given it to an agent who has kept it in a personal trust account, you can demand it back, and in most cases the agent will immediately return it (perhaps risking the ire of the seller). If the conditions of the purchase agreement can't be fulfilled, normally you're entitled to get it back, and most agents don't want to argue the point.

On the other hand, if the deposit's been placed in an escrow account, it usually takes both the buyer's and the seller's agreement to get it out.

Maybe the seller is angry that the deal fell through and says, "I'm not signing anything." There your deposit sits, even though you're perfectly entitled to it. Unless the agent can prevail and convince the seller to release it, it could remain there for a long time!

As a practical matter, however, as soon as another buyer comes along, the seller probably will be forced to release it so as not to jeopardize a later sale.

All of which brings us back to my original point. The money you put up for deposit is at risk. The less you put up, the less you risk.

What Are Contingencies?

A contingency clause is essentially any clause in a contract that says the offer depends or hinges on some other event or action. For example, wording that would say, "This offer is contingent upon the buyer winning the state lottery" is a kind of contingency clause, one that obviously no sane seller would accept.

I once knew a builder whose advice was, "No matter what the contract, always be sure that somewhere in it, it says, 'subject to.' I don't care what comes after the 'subject to,' just as long as it's in there." The words "subject to" have essentially the same meaning as "contingent." They make the sales offer hinge on some event or action. What my builder friend meant was that as long as those words were in it, he could get out of the contract if he had to. He had many experiences fighting subcontractors, landowners, and others, and I firmly believe to this day that he could get out of any contract with those words in it. For your purposes, however, a contingency clause is very useful to protect you against an unforeseen change of condition.

Some contingencies are absolutely desirable for the sales agreement and few agents would hesitate to put them in. Typical contingency clauses include:

Common Contingency Clauses

- Financing—If you can't get the financing you need, there is no deal and you get your deposit back.
- Disclosures—You have the right to approve the seller's property disclosures. Don't approve them and there's no deal.
- Professional Inspection—You have the right to approve a professional inspection report. Don't approve it and the deal's off.

Of course, there may be some other contingency that you need added to the deal.

TRAP—THE MORE CONTINGENCIES, THE LESS LIKELY THE SELLER WILL ACCEPT THE DEAL

The more you protect yourself with contingencies, the less the seller is going to want to sign your offer. After all, if you make it full of contingencies, it's like Swiss cheese; it holds little water and you could slip out of the deal at your pleasure.

What About a Pending Sale Contingency?

Here you make your offer contingent on the sale of your current home, which is already in escrow. If your current home falls out of escrow, then you're not committed to move forward with the new deal. You could also make the sale of your new home contingent, even if you haven't yet found a buyer for your old one.

In a cold market, sometimes sellers who are desperate will accept this contingency. In a good market, however, most won't. They realize they are tying the sale of their house to the sale of someone else's house. It's like having to make two deals instead of one.

What About a Frivolous Contingency?

As noted, you can make the deal contingent on almost anything, from the occurrence of sunspots to your winning the Irish Sweepstakes. However, don't expect a seller to be thrilled about these. The more frivolous your contingencies appear, the less likely you are to get the seller to accept your offer.

Who Should Write the Contingency?

Some purchase agreements have the most common contingencies already written in. Your agent simply checks the appropriate box and the contingency is in effect. Of course, you may want to have your attorney check the language used in the agreement.

If a new contingency is to be written, it should be handled by an attorney. This does not mean that a good agent can't do it. Many agents with years of experience can handle these easily. Even so, it wouldn't hurt to have an attorney recheck it, just to be sure.

What Terms Should I Offer?

The terms of a purchase can sometimes be more important than the price. (Terms are often structured in the form of a contingency; see above.)

Sellers are often hung up on price. Offer them their full price and they may give you ridiculously favorable terms. For example, to get their price, the sellers just might be willing to finance the sale (carry back a mortgage). If you're having credit problems, it's something to consider.

What Are Time Terms?

There are other terms you might consider. One of the most crucial is time. How long do you have to secure financing, to come up with the down payment and closing costs, to close the escrow?

Time is often negotiated. Perhaps the seller wants 90 days before moving out. That suits you fine, so there is immediate agreement

On the other hand, perhaps the seller wants to close escrow in 30 days, but you feel you'll need 90 to raise the cash for the down payment.

Now time is a negotiating point. You compromise. You'll take a chance on coming up with the cash in 60 days, but the seller has to be willing to lower the price $1000 or throw in the refrigerator.

The seller balks and says the most he can go is 45 days, but he'll lower the interest rate on the second mortgage he's carrying from 9 percent to 8 percent and throw in the refrigerator. Is it okay with you?

Now you have to make a judgment call. The agent may suggest a "bridge" loan (temporary financing until you can get your cash) to cover the extra time you'll need. But this costs you extra money.

In the final analysis, you'll have to weigh all the factors regarding time. Just remember it's a negotiating card, one that you can play.

What Are Other Terms?

There are a host of other common terms in a real estate transaction, almost all of which are negotiable. For example, you may agree to pay full price for a property *if* the seller agrees to pay your closing costs.

Or you'll buy only if the seller agrees to pay for a special mold and mildew inspection (offered by some termite and fungus infestation removal companies) as well as any repair work removing black mold.

Or . . . ?

Unfortunately, throughout all of this bargaining you're going to have to pretty much rely on yourself. Certainly your agent will be there to try to protect you.

However, if you want some particularly onerous terms (to the seller), your agent might not be too happy, as it could make it harder to get the sellers to sign. And I've never met an agent who wanted to work harder closing a deal.

Thus, it's up to you to get the best terms.

As noted earlier, the time to consult an attorney is before you need one. At this juncture a real estate attorney can prove extremely useful. The attorney can create a purchase agreement that protects you and provides the most favorable terms (for you).

TRAP—THE ATTORNEY PITFALL

Beware of attorneys who work too hard for your interests. In general, real estate agents dread attorneys, not because they don't protect people, but because they tend to muck up deals. There's an old saying among real estate agents that the fastest way to have a deal go sour is to bring in an attorney. Yes, you want your rights protected and you want the most favorable terms. But you also want to be able ultimately to purchase the house. An attorney can create a sales contract so favorable to you that no seller will accept it. As with the ancient Greeks, moderation is in order. Allow your attorney to draw up the terms correctly and to advise. But also rely on common sense.

When Do You Get Possession?

The question here is: When will you take possession of the property? The most common answer is at the close of escrow after title has been recorded in your name.

The danger with occupancy is that the sellers won't move out. There are many reasons the sellers might not move. A new house they are planning to move into might not be ready. Or there might be illness in the family, and a family member might not be easily moved. Or they could just be ornery.

Whatever the reason, if they don't move, it spells trouble for you. If the sellers are still in possession of the house once you get title, you can't easily have them removed. (In the old days "self-help eviction" was allowed—you could physically go in and throw them out! That's been a taboo for quite a few decades now.)

To get the sellers out you might need to conduct an "unlawful detainer" action through the courts——eviction. This usually takes at least a month, may cost upwards of $1000 in costs, and usually requires the services of an attorney.

TIP—THE SIMPLE WAY TO AVOID OCCUPANCY PROBLEMS

There's an easy way to help ensure that there is no problem with occupancy. Be sure that the purchase agreement specifies that the sellers are to be out by the time escrow closes, preferably at least one day in advance of the close. Then, before signing all of the loan documents that buyers usually sign, check to see that the sellers have complied. If the property is empty, it's a good sign that the sellers are out, and you're free to sign. If they're not out, it could be a problem, and you may not want to sign—check with your agent and attorney.

On the other hand, there are extenuating circumstances. You may want to move in early to get your kids registered in school. The sellers may want to move out late, so their kids don't have to switch schools midterm.

In these situations, a rental agreement can be arranged. If you move in early (assuming the property is already empty), you pay the seller's rent. If they stay late, they pay you rent.

TRAP—TENANT AGREEMENTS CAN LEAD TO PROBLEMS

Let's say the sellers want to stay after the close of escrow, after ownership transfers to you. They then become tenants with all the rights that tenants have. They might not move as agreed. They might leave the property a mess. You can somewhat reduce these problems by having the sellers sign a strong tenant's agreement, along with rent sufficient to make your monthly payment, and a hefty security deposit to cover breakage and cleaning. However, if they refuse to move as agreed, you might still need to have them evicted.

Should I Insist on a Final Walk-Through?

You see the property before you make the offer. The offer's made and accepted. Then there's a wait of a month or so while financing is arranged, title is cleared, and so forth. Now you're ready to close the deal. *But* how do you know that the property is now in the same condition as when you first saw it? How do you know the seller hasn't smashed holes in the walls and broken the appliances? (Unlikely, but it does happen.) How do you know there aren't scratches on the floor, damaged sinks and toilets, and so on?

You know by insisting that the purchase agreement gives you the right to a final walk-through inspection. Before the deal closes, you once again examine what you are buying to be sure it's as you first saw it (or reasonably close).

TRAP—IT'S NOT TIME TO RENEGOTIATE THE DEAL

It's important to understand that a final walk-through is not supposed to be an opportunity for you to reconsider your purchase or reopen negotiations. It is just supposed to be a chance for you to examine the property to see that it's as it was when you originally made your offer. Most savvy sellers will include a clause stating that if something of consequence is found wrong, the sellers have the right to correct it—that the final walk-through is not intended to be a new beginning in negotiating price or terms.

TIP—SOMETIMES YOU'LL WANT TO RENEGOTIATE

Nonetheless, buyers have used faults found on the final inspection to attempt to back out of a deal at the last minute. (Their reasons can vary from finding a serious fault in the property, to finding another more preferable house.) My suggestion is that if you want to renegotiate based on the final walk-though, you better have found some serious problem with the house, or else you'll have an angry seller to contend with.

Sometimes agents will suggest that a specific date for the final walk-through be written into the purchase agreement. I feel this is usually a bad idea. You don't want a specific set date because you don't know when escrow will close and you'll get occupancy. I prefer that the final inspection should be set as close to the day escrow closes as possible, preferably a day or two before.

Keep in mind that if you inspect the property too early, the sellers might still be living in it, and furniture and carpets not yet removed might conceal potential damage. Try to be sure the sellers are out before you have your final inspection. (This also helps solve the problem of occupancy noted above.)

TIP—KEEP UTILITIES ON

Be sure the gas, electricity, and water are on when you have your "walk-through" inspection. Otherwise, you won't be able to tell if any of the house's systems are broken.

TRAP—EXPECT DIRT AND MINOR DAMAGE

Don't expect the property to look as clean as it did when you first saw it. If the seller was living in the property when you first saw it, carpets and furniture hid a lot of marks and scuffing. Once the furniture and carpeting are removed, these stand out like sore thumbs. Dark scratch marks on walls and scrapes on floors are common. Indentations in carpeting where heavy furniture stood are also common, as is some slight discoloration. (Most of this carpet indentation will tend to disappear within a few days on its own.)

What you need to look for is any significant breakage, damage, or other condition that was not there when you first saw the home or when you had your professional home inspection. Also, check for any damaged or broken items that the seller did not disclose in the sales agreement or accompanying documents.

What specifically should you look for?

Items to Watch Out for in a Final Walk-Through

- Holes in wall, broken plaster
- Broken windows
- Inoperative or broken appliances such as stove, garbage disposal, and oven

- Faulty or broken water heater (as evidenced by no hot water), gas heater, or air conditioner. Check to see that the heater heats and the air conditioner cools.

- Gashes, slashes, or marks in wood floors that will require redoing the floor

- Damaged or inoperative light fixtures

- Broken or inoperative heating or air-conditioning thermostat

- Leaky plumbing, as evidenced by new water marks or water on floors

- Faults in the electrical system, as evidenced by light switches or wall plugs that don't work

- New damage to carpet, such as dirt or, most important, cat or dog urination. I've seen sellers who let their pets run loose in the house after the sales agreement was signed, figuring that it wasn't their problem any more. But if you accept a carpet that has been ruined by urination, it's a big problem for you. Odor is usually the giveaway. If you suspect a problem, don't hesitate to get down on your hands and knees to check it out. Better to discover it now than when you're the owner.

TRAP—PET ODOR MAY BE PERMANENT

I have found that urination from pets *cannot* be effectively removed from carpeting. Typically the carpeting and usually the pad underneath (and sometimes even the flooring!) must be replaced. An entire house's carpeting might need to be replaced to match a small area of damage. I won't accept a carpet problem caused by pets. Insist that it be fixed, even if that requires the sellers to recarpet the entire house. (Be sure you approve the quality of carpeting and padding they use.)

What About a Professional Home Inspection?

Yes, you should have it for your own protection. There's an entire chapter devoted to what you should look for (Chapter 13). Just remember that in most cases, the buyer pays for the inspection and it costs around $300. But it may very well turn out to be money well spent.

Should I Insist on a Home Protection Plan?

Several national and some local companies offer plans that give you some insurance protection for the major systems of your home. Typically they cover plumbing (including water heater), heating, air conditioning, electrical, appliances, and so forth. The idea is that for a set period of time after you move in (usually one year), should there be a problem, the home protection company will cover it (minus a small deductible). The cost is usually nominal, a few hundred dollars for a year's worth of coverage.

In most purchases the sellers pay for the plan; you pay the deductible (usually under $50) for each time you call someone out to deal with a problem. Most plans are renewable, so if you like the one you've got, you can keep it. (Of course, you'll have to pay for it after the first year!)

The home protection plan should be included as part of the purchase agreement. The agreement should state that it will be purchased at the time of sale, and that the seller will provide the appropriate warranties. (The seller is usually required to verify that everything is in working condition before the plan takes effect.) If you wait until after title transfers, you either may not be able to get the plan or may find that *you* have to warrant the condition of the various home systems only to discover that some aren't working!

Should I Agree to an Arbitration Clause?

Some sales agreements contain arbitration clauses. Typically these refer only to the deposit, but in some cases they may refer to other areas. Basically what they say is that if there is a disagreement, you will submit it to binding arbitration—you will go along with whatever an arbitrator says.

Keep in mind that you could be giving up significant rights if you sign an arbitration agreement. If the seller refuses to go through with the deal after you've made all sorts of commitments (from accepting a new job, to putting your kids in a new school, to moving across the country) you're likely to be quite upset. You might want the right to sue for damages.

However, you could lose the option of suing the seller for damages or specific performance (forcing them to sell to you) by signing this clause. (On the other hand, the sellers could be giving up the same rights, meaning that you could be avoiding the risk of being sued.) It's a good idea to ask your attorney about this clause.

If you agree to arbitration, just remember that for it to be effective, both you (the buyer) and the seller have to agree. If just one agrees, it won't work.

Also, be sure you know who the arbitrator will be. Many arbitration clauses specify that the arbitrator will be a member of the American Arbitration Association (local members are listed in the yellow pages of your phone book). This is fine, since such members are skilled at arbitration. But they are also quite expensive. It really doesn't make much sense to use an arbitrator when his or her fee may exceed the worth of the item being arbitrated.

Do I Understand Prorations?

Typically there are always some items that are "prorated," such as taxes, fire insurance, or interest on a mortgage you might be assuming. This means they are adjusted based on who owes them.

For example, a fire insurance policy is typically written and paid for at least one year in advance. However, the house may be sold after the policy has been in effect for only three months. You, the buyer, may be taking over the policy. In this case the seller will undoubtedly want to "prorate" the cost of the insurance policy. In other words, you would pay the seller back for the nine months you are going to be using the policy.

The same applies to prepaid taxes or taxes that are due.

Adjustments are made in your favor or the seller's favor, depending on when payment was made and what the date of proration is.

There are usually only two questions with regard to proration: what will be prorated and on what date? Typically all items that are affected by time are prorated. Usually the proration date is the close of escrow.

Should I Write in Personal Property That Goes with the Sale?

When you purchase a home, you are basically buying "real property." Loosely defined, real property is the land, the house, and anything that's permanently attached to it. For example, the windows in the house are real property.

Personal property, on the other hand, is everything else. Furniture is personal property, as are dishes, clothes, and most things that you can take with you.

For most things the definition of what's personal and what's real property is easily grasped and readily agreed to. However, in some circumstances the line between personal and real becomes very fine, and that's when you can run into trouble.

For example, wall-to-wall carpeting that is tacked down is normally considered real property—it's permanently attached to the house. But what about a rug that is thrown over the floor and not attached? Normally, it would be considered personal property.

Drapes that are hung on rods are usually considered personal property, if you can take them off without in any way damaging the house. But the rods that hold the drapes and that are affixed by screws into the walls of the house may be considered real property.

Can you see where problems could arise? You see a house and you fall in love with it. It is completely carpeted with throw rugs and drapes. You buy it. But on your final walk-through, all the carpeting is gone, as are the drapes. What happened?

Why, the seller remarks innocently, those were my personal property and I took them along with the furniture. Is the seller allowed to do that? Probably, if the items weren't permanently attached and if no mention of them was made in the sales agreement.

Don't assume anything when it comes to items such as rugs, drapes, and even appliances. (Yes, appliances! Most so-called built-in stoves and ovens just pull out and unplug. Unless they are included in a sales agreement, a seller may feel they are personal property too!) Assume they are personal property unless you are specifically told they are not.

It is because of the confusion between personal and real property that today most sales agreements include a clause which states that all appliances, wall coverings, and floor coverings are included with the purchase, "except____," and a space is left to write in any exceptions. A separate clause may include all appliances and light fixtures. Look for these clauses in the sales agreement, and if they are not there, ask your agent and/or attorney why they are not.

TIP—GET A BETTER DEAL BY ADDING PERSONAL PROPERTY

What should be fairly obvious is that the distinction between personal and real property has many gray areas. Sometimes you can take advantage of these in-between spots. For example, you look at a house and you are impressed with the kitchen. It has had a makeover and is truly beautiful. There are impressive oak cabinets and a special wall cabinet into which a large two-door refrigerator fits perfectly. You ask about the refrigerator and are told that it, of course, is the personal property of the seller. It's not included in the sale. But, you think to yourself, where in the world am I ever going to find another refrigerator to fit so perfectly in there? Isn't it a shame that it doesn't go with the house. Well, of course, you can make it go with the house. When you write up your offer to purchase, indicate that one of the conditions of sale is that the refrigerator goes with the house. No refrigerator, no deal. Will the sellers accept? It depends on how anxious they are to sell. If you're the first serious buyer to come along in months, they'll probably grab it.

Pay Careful Attention to Your Purchase Agreement

The purchase agreement is where you make your deal (good, bad, or mediocre) and define how the purchase process will be followed until the house is yours. Take time with the purchase agreement and make sure that you understand it thoroughly.

Check with your agent and attorney. Be sure you're getting all that you can. Be sure you're making the best deal possible.

11
Finding Fixer-Uppers

A "fixer" is short for "fixer-upper" (also sometimes called a "handy-man's special"). It's a house (or condo/co-op) that is in less than perfect condition, sometimes far less. Some merely need paint. Others need a complete makeover. Some even require structural repair. Whatever their deficiencies, they are typically sold at a discount.

If you're having trouble finding a home you can afford to buy in the neighborhood you want, then one alternative may be to consider a fixer. Here you can sometimes substitute "sweat equity" for the cash (or credit/income for loan qualifying) that you need to get in.

Why Should I Consider a Fixer?

There are three reasons that people want to buy fixers. They are:

- Get into an area you'd otherwise not be able to afford
- Get into a house you'd otherwise not be able to afford
- Make a profit

TIP—IT'S NOT SIMPLY COSMETIC

My wife and I have a running battle over what constitutes a fixer. She feels that if the paint isn't new and there are one or two cracked counter tiles, it's a fixer. I, on the other hand, maintain that the property has to have a big enough problem that no one will pay full price for it—obsolete kitchen/bath, broken doors in interior, cracked foundation, and so on. Her complaint is that no one will come down on the price for what she considers a fixer. Mine is that they often won't come down far enough to make buying the home and fixing it worthwhile.

Who Should *Not* Consider a Fixer

It's important to understand at the onset that if you're going to buy a fixer, even if you get it dirt cheap, it's going to cost you time, money, and effort to renovate it. It would be a mistake to buy such a property thinking you can simply move in as you would a house that's already in perfect shape.

If you're the sort that looks at homes and tends to like those that are "ready to go," then chances are you would not be happy with a fixer. In fact, you'd probably walk away from a perfect "fixer" steal simply because you wouldn't recognize it.

Recognizing a Fixer

As suggested previously, fixers run the gamut of those that simply need cosmetic work to those that are in such bad shape they need to be "scraped" (demolished) and a new house erected from scratch.

While most of us would prefer to stay closer to the cosmetic realm, where cleaning, painting, and replacing fixtures is about all we'd be called upon to do, the big discounts come from properties that have more serious problems. For example, at the more serious end of fixers are homes that have broken foundations, that have collapsing roofs, that have been condemned because of fires or ground shifting, that are sliding down hills and on and on. Homes that have problems this serious will obviously come with a strong discount. Indeed, you may be able to pick up the property for just the cost of the land. In some cases, that's less than half the price for a home in good condition.

Cosmetics versus Renovation in a Fixer

You've got a cosmetic fixer IF:

- Paint will handle most of the problems
- New carpeting will do the trick
- Landscaping the front will be the finishing touch

You've got a renovation fixer IF:

- You need to put in a new kitchen and/or bath
- There are structural problems with the roof, foundation or framing
- Major systems (plumbing, heating, electrical) need repair

However, fixing such calamitous problems requires ingenuity, money, nerve, and stick-to-itness. Unless you have all four, plus a pretty strong background in renovation, my suggestion is that you simply stay away from these. If it's your the first time out, you could get burned badly on one of them.

Rather, what you probably want is something closer to the cosmetic fixer. You want a home that looks like a mess but can be shaped up with lots of paint, simple fixing, and TLC. Do such fixers exist?

TIP—KNOW THINE OWN ABILITIES

Perhaps the most important thing when evaluating a fixer is to determine whether you can do the work yourself, or whether it's beyond you. For this reason, it's always a good idea to call in experts—contractors, engineers, agents—people who specialize in fixing the particular problem. In many cases they'll simply give you a bid. In others you may have to pay them a fee. But either way, very often only they can tell you how the problem can be correctly fixed. And how much that will realistically cost.

Where Can I Find a Fixer?

Fixers abound in all communities and in every part of the country. They come about because some people simply never maintain or repair their home. They let it run down until it's time to sell . . . and then it's a fixer.

Other times it's a case where you have an older home and/or an older owner. The older the home, the more maintenance and repair. The older the owner, the less likely the person is to do this. In some cases the owners die and their property is then disposed of through probate. You can sometimes get a terrific fixer deal in that way.

Other owners who lose their jobs, get a divorce, or otherwise run into circumstances where they can't keep up the mortgage, lose their property to foreclosure. You can sometimes buy a terrific fixer from a bank or other lender that's an REO (Real Estate Owned). (For more detailed information on probate sales and REOs, check into *Finding Hidden Real Estate Bargains* by my favorite author.)

And, of course, you can work with agents.

TIP—SEPARATING WHEAT FROM CHAFF

The trick is identifying a fixer that has potential.

Should I Work With Agents?

Agents are always on the lookout for fixers, and if they know that's what you want, most will look for you. However, don't expect agents to fall over at your feet if you tell them you specifically want a fixer. Agents know that good fixers seldom come along, and completing a deal on them often takes lots more work than selling a ready-to-go house.

Check the MLS® (Multiple Listing Service), which your Realtor® should be able to access. This can take time and careful scouting. However, today the MLS is computerized in almost all areas of the country. You can simply sit down with your agent and use his or her computer's search engine to hunt for suitable properties.

Tips for Finding Fixers on the MLS

Pull the lowest-priced properties in each neighborhood. Check for expressions on the listing such as, "Needs tender loving care," or "sweat equity opportunity."

Carefully examine the picture. Almost all listings today come with at least one good color image. Does the house look dazzling, as many a fixed-up place will? Or does it look a bit tired? Look especially for tall weeds in the front yard, big cracks in the driveway, and temporary cyclone fences. All indicate a problem house.

Check out the "aged" listings. The longer a house has been on the market, the more likely that it has problems. Besides, sellers of homes that have just been listed are unlikely to consider taking price cuts. Usually a seller won't want to reduce the price until a home has sat unsold for a minimum of 60 days or longer.

Ask your agent for help. He or she may well know the area you want to live in. The agent can read the listing, look at the picture, and if they've visited the place, give you a quick synopsis of the home's condition.

Check the "expireds." If you don't find anything suitable with the current listings, ask to see those listings that have expired. The MLS also carries information on listings that have expired without being sold. This can be a real treasure trove. Listings that have expired are no longer listed for sale. However, often the owners are still willing to sell them. It's just that they've gotten discouraged and have taken the home off the market, often just temporarily. Ask yourself, why did the listing expire? If it was a sharp house, it should have sold, unless the price was unrealistic. Often the reason a home didn't sell is because it's a fixer.

Take your time. Be sure you go through *all* of the listings. If you're in a metropolitan area that has thousands of listings, it could take days, sometimes a week. But if you find a good fixer, it will be time well spent.

Other Sources of Fixers

Sometimes there are FSBO fixers (FSBO stands for "For Sale By Owner"). A FSBO seller wants to tell you they've got the perfect fixer. But it's not listed. So perhaps they've taken an ad in the local newspaper. Perhaps they've put the home on a Web site, maybe even their own. Or perhaps they've written it up on a 4-x-6 card and posted it at a local grocery or drug store.

Where you get the information is irrelevant. I once bought a fixer after meeting the relative of a seller who was sitting next to me on a plane ride between Oakland and Los Angeles! We got to talking, she told me about the house, I made arrangements to see it, the seller and I agreed on a price, and within 30 days I owned it!

How Do I Evaluate a Fixer?

Once you've found it, the next question you must answer is, "How much work is required?" That's a lot harder to do than it may at first seem. The reason is that you have to get two important figures. The first is the value of the property after it's finished, totally fixed up.

The second is the amount of money it's going to cost you to do the fixing. Here's the best formula I've found for determining the amount you should offer on a fixer:

Formua for Making a Fixer Offer

Value if in perfect shape	$200,000
Less cost of fixing up	−50,000
Less your time and/or profit	−25,000
Your offer	125,000

When you think about it, this only makes sense. It's going to cost you money to fix up the property. And it's only fair that you factor in your time/profit.

TRAP—YOU ARE WORTH IT!

Don't make the classic mistake of thinking your time isn't valuable. It is. If not spent working on the fixer, you could be earning money elsewhere, or at the very least, relaxing with your family!

TIP—YOUR COSTS WILL VARY

 The cost to fix up depends heavily on how much of the work you do yourself and how much you hire out. My suggestion is that when determining how much to offer, you always base this on hiring everything out. That way in case you err, you'll at least not be erring on paying too much for the property. If you later do much, if not all, of the work yourself, your savings will be that much more.

How Much Will It Cost to Fix Up?

There is an apparent contradiction in the fact that the house that looks the worst, a cosmetic fixer, often costs the most. The trouble arises from the fact that today sellers are sophisticated enough to know that cosmetic fixes are cheap and easy to repair, and they simply don't want to give up any of their profits. Often, in order to get a really good deal, you'll have to buy a house with very serious problems. Of course, that may be simply biting off more than you can chew.

One excellent method here is to line up a series of people in the construction industry who are willing to come out and give you advice. You would, hopefully, have at least the following:

Advisors You Might Need

- Carpenter/general contractor
- Plumber
- Electrician
- Roofer
- Carpet layer
- Painter
- Mason (for driveways, paths, foundations)

The problem is getting them to come out and look over a property that you don't yet own. You want them to give you advice, maybe a bid, *before* you buy. In fact, their input will help you to make the purchase decision.

However, their time is scarce and they may be hesitant to come out and give you a bid on a "maybe." That's why it's important to contact these people in advance and try to gain their confidence. Tell them that you plan on using them. If not on this house (because you didn't buy it), then the next one. If they won't budge, and you absolutely need a quick opinion, you might have to pay for their time. Offer them 50 to 100 bucks to come out. Yes, it goes against the rules to pay for a bid, but if you need information fast, it can be the right thing to do.

Can I Line Up the Financing?

Financing a fixer can be tricky. Lenders won't want to give you prime loans on a property that's in bad shape. But some lenders will give you subprime loans. You'll have to scout this out. Your best bet will be banks and the few mortgage brokers (if you can fine one) who specialize in fixers.

TIP—GET THE MONEY UP FRONT

 The cardinal rule for financing a fixer is to line up *all* the money you'll need in advance. The reason is that once you get started tearing out walls and flooring, it will be far harder to convince any lender to give you a loan. This means you'll have to calculate pretty closely just how much money it will take to do the entire fix-up.

The Hardest Part

Probably the hardest part of buying a fixer is getting the seller to accept a reasonable price. (Refer to our earlier formula for determining how much to pay.)

Sellers have heard that property prices have gone up. And they want to participate on the boom. Of course, they don't want to realistically discount their property because of the poor shape it's in.

All of which is to say, plan on doing lots of negotiation. And plan on making lots of lowball offers, most of which won't be accepted.

Just be sure that you don't get discouraged and offer more than you should for a property. Once you make your calculations, don't redo them upward because a seller won't budge. Stick with them. Better to lose a deal than to get stuck by paying too much and not being able to fix it up to a market price.

Don't get discouraged. Lots of people find, buy, and successfully fix up properties every day. There's no good reason you can't be one of them.

12
Buying Directly from Builders and Saving

Perhaps you are considering the purchase of a new home instead of a resale. Are there different things to watch for? Are there special benefits as well as pitfalls to avoid?

While there are similarities, buying a new home is substantially different from buying a resale. It is a different market that requires you to have specialized knowledge.

Will a New Home or a Resale Appreciate Faster?

A question frequently asked by buyers is: "Where will I get the greatest appreciation—in a new home or in a resale?" (Or in a bad market, which home holds up its value the best?) To put it another way: "If I had a choice between two houses, a brand new one and a resale each worth $200,000 and both in similar neighborhoods, which house would make me the most money or cost me the least money over the next five years?"

In the distant past the answer was generally the resale. The existing house had developed neighborhoods, schools, shopping, parks, and so on. It had all the amenities already in place, and for that reason resales tended to appreciate more than new homes . . . and to cost more as well.

During the last quarter of the twentieth century, however, the tables turned. Then, in many areas of the country (but not all), the

139

price appreciation on new homes was far and away greater than on resales. Good advice at the time was to simply buy a new home and ride the wave of appreciation up to profits.

New or Resale?

Buy a new home IF:
- If you don't want to inherit maintenance and repair problems
- If you want to move into a "clean" house
- If you don't mind putting in back yards, fences, and otherwise completing the development of the property

Buy a resale IF:
- If you want to live in a "proven" neighborhood (established schools, crime rates, and so on)
- If you desire a mature area (lots of trees and shrubs)
- Want "character"—Victorian, New England, Spanish, Plantation, or other style

---

With the depressed real estate market of the early 1990s, buyers discovered that it didn't matter if a house was new or old, it could go down in value. Only those homes in the very best neighborhoods, new or old, kept their value or appreciated.

Today, in the twenty-first century, both new homes and resales are moving ahead rapidly in price. So which to buy?

Consider Neighborhood

A resale has a proven neighborhood—you know what it looks like. A new home only has a hoped-for neighborhood. Maybe it will turn out great . . . and maybe not.

If it were me, I would shop neighborhood first.

Consider Lot Size

Land is the single most expensive part of a home. Therefore, to conserve on land, today's builders often put large homes on postage stamp-sized lots. If you like a lot of privacy and space, consider a resale. The older home usually will offer you more land.

Consider Home Size

On the other hand, newer homes tends to be far larger than their earlier cousins. Today's buyer wants a larger home. And the feeling seems to be, "Who cares about a small lot, as long as I have a big house?"

TIP—BUYING LATER IN A NEW DEVELOPMENT CAN PAY OFF

Many new developments are built in phases. If the initial phase is successful (a good neighborhood), the later phases usually turn out similar. If you can get a later-phase home at an earlier-phase price, you could be headed for a profit-making deal.

Real estate is a localized market. That means that you cannot say that something is true at any given time for all parts of the country. While Southern California, for example, or New York may see property values skyrocket, at the same time parts of the Midwest or South may see them stagnate . . . or vice versa.

How Do I Find the Right New Home?

If you're determined to buy a new home, be prepared to spend some time looking. In most areas of the country, the era of the huge tract has given way to smaller, condensed tracts built a phase at a time.

To see all of the new homes in your area, you may have to spend time traveling. Many areas have a "buyer's guide" to new homes—a small magazine detailing the houses and their price range and showing maps of how to get there. The Sunday real estate section of any major newspaper almost always has ads for new homes.

What Should I Look For in a New Home?

Here's a checklist of items to look for when choosing a brand-new home:

New Home Checklist

Number of bedrooms. Three or four is often best for resale, two may restrict your ability to resell quickly, five could make the house overbuilt for the area._____

Number of bathrooms. Two is minimal, three is better, four could be overkill._____

Ceilings. High ceilings are in vogue. A better house will have at least one room with vaulted ceilings, usually a living or family room._____

Kitchen. Large and well-equipped kitchens sell houses. If your kitchen has an island in it complete with a stove, all the better. Is the oven self-cleaning?_____

Garage. A two-car garage is a must. Three-car is better._____

Additional rooms. These are a plus, if they don't force the price out of sight. They include library, nursery, computer room, even a home theater._____

Yard. Small yards are the rule today, given the high cost of land. Many families actually prefer small yards to avoid having to do extensive yard work. People with children, however, usually like larger yards. Large yards are considered luxury items and are found in more expensive homes._____

Central air conditioning. More and more it is considered to be a necessity, rather than a luxury._____

High-quality insulation. Check with the builder. The "R" rating should be the minimum required for the weather in your area. Higher "R" ratings will decrease your heating and cooling costs. Ask if the house was "wrapped" with a vapor/moisture barrier. It helps the insulation do its work._____

Glass. Are the sliding-glass doors, bathroom windows, and other windows that are easily accessed by children made of "safety glass?"_____? Are they double-pane?_____? Low-E_____?

Electrical outlets. The standard in most construction is one outlet every 12 feet of linear wall space. Extra outlets in kitchens and baths are a plus._____?

Floor coverings. Wall-to-wall carpet is the rule in most new homes. Tiles are a plus. Hardwood floors are an additional plus, but remember, you'll probably want to buy carpet to put over them._____?

How Do I Check Out a Neighborhood

It's hard with a new home because frequently the neighborhood is likewise new and undeveloped. Here's a checklist to help you evaluate a neighborhood for a new home.

New-Home Neighborhood Checklist

	YES	NO
■ Are the local schools good? (You can ask to see their scores on standardized tests to judge.)	[ ]	[ ]
■ Are the schools nearby?	[ ]	[ ]
■ Are there day-care facilities nearby?	[ ]	[ ]
■ Is the area relatively crime free? (Check with the police department's Public Affairs officer, who can usually give you crime statistics down to the block.)	[ ]	[ ]
■ Does the police department seem responsive?	[ ]	[ ]
■ Is there adequate fire protection? (Check with your insurance company for fire ratings in the area.)	[ ]	[ ]
■ Is shopping nearby?	[ ]	[ ]
■ Is there a hospital nearby?	[ ]	[ ]
■ Is the neighborhood "quiet"? (Come back at different times of the day to check.)	[ ]	[ ]
■ Are posted speed limits slow? (You want a 25 mph limit, not 35 or 45.)	[ ]	[ ]
■ Is there a high-traffic street nearby that cars shoot out of?	[ ]	[ ]
■ Is there a park nearby?	[ ]	[ ]
■ Is public transportation available?	[ ]	[ ]
■ Is there adequate off-street parking?	[ ]	[ ]
■ Are the lots "private" enough?	[ ]	[ ]
■ Is the tract landscaped?	[ ]	[ ]
■ Is there danger of future erosion? (If you're not sure, check with a soils engineer.)	[ ]	[ ]

- Does the water system provide pure drinking water? (The water company almost always must supply you with the results of water purity testing.)   [ ]   [ ]
- Are there any special assessments that you'll have to pay (Street improvement, sewer tax, and so on)?   [ ]   [ ]
- Are there any nearby hazards or nuisances (Factories, swamps or rivers, oil tanks, hazardous waste facilities, and so on)?   [ ]   [ ]
- Are the homes connected to a sewer system (septic systems are less desirable)?   [ ]   [ ]

In addition to the features of the house itself as well as the neighborhood, there is the factor of the new home market. The housing market is volatile, with many ups and downs. Here's what to look for.

How Do I Judge the New-House Market

In a slow market (no rapid price appreciation, but no falling prices, either), there are sometimes more new homes than buyers, and builders are anxious to sell them off. The ads for the homes are placed in all papers, there are signs along the major roads directing you to the new tracts, and there are almost always models of all the homes available to see.

TIP—NEW HOMES ARE CHEAPER TO OPERATE

As a rule, new homes will have newer and more efficient heating and cooling systems, more insulation, better windows (double pane and low-E), tighter weather stripping, and so on. This all translates into lower energy costs.

While the salespeople in the office try to get you to make a quick decision, remember that you usually have plenty of time. You can leisurely shop around, going from model to model until you find just the right home for you. Once you find it, you can often negotiate more favorable terms from the builder (reduced price, a buy-down on the loan—where the builder pays part of your interest for a few years—free amenities such as fences, yards, and so forth).

This is the ideal market in which to buy a new home. In a sense, it's almost a "buyer's market," and you're sitting in the driver's seat.

TIP—SMALL HOUSE, TOP LOCATION

Try to find a small to medium-sized home in the best-located tract—this property will often appreciate the fastest. (Beware the very smallest home, as it may be simply too small for many buyers when it comes time for you to sell; the largest home is often too expensive when it comes time for resale.)

What If We're in a Real Estate Recession?

A real estate recession happens rarely, but it does happen. You'll know a depressed market if you're in it. Every Sunday the paper will offer "repos" and "REOs" and "bank-owned properties" for sale or auction. If the ads don't alert you, there are other signs of a down market:

How to Recognize a Real Estate Recession

- Statistics available from brokers and published in the business section of the local papers indicate that the volume of home sales is dramatically down from the previous year.
- The number of houses advertised for sale (both new and resale) in the newspapers is enormous.
- The price of homes is declining. This is usually measured by the median price. Instead of going up, statistics may suggest it's declining.
- Government home auctions by the FHA (Federal Housing Administration) or the VA (Veterans Administration) may be held weekly, as evidenced by large ads in local papers.
- There's difficulty getting financing from lenders because of the many houses already in default.

■ Tracts of new homes are fully built with the houses standing vacant and unsold.

TIP—DON'T BUY NEW ON THE WAY DOWN

Be wary of buying a new home in a real estate recession. In a down market you can find apparent "steals" on resales as desperate sellers fight to get out. However, how wise is it to buy today when you can buy the same house for less tomorrow?

What About Buying a New Home When the Market's Hot?

A hot market can be the most difficult time to buy a home. Hot markets have occurred on both coasts at various times over the past 50 years, the most recent starting around 1998 or 1999, depending on your area of the country.

What happens in a hot market is that there are more buyers than there are homes available for sale, both resales and new. (Part of the reason is that prices are perceived to be going up, and speculators enter the market. Also, there may be a shortage of homes in your area of the country—something that has occurred, for example, in Southern California and elsewhere.)

TIP—FOLLOW INTEREST RATES

If you're concerned about the market, be sure to check interest rates regularly. When they are falling, it's almost a sure sign that soon, if not already, prices will likely rise. When they are rising, watch out. Real estate does not like higher interest rates, and a slowdown could be imminent.

In a hot market, prices go up for both resales and new homes. When you are seeking a new home in a hot market, the odds are set against you. You are competing against other buyers for relatively few homes. Builders don't need to advertise, since buyers are beating the woods looking for new homes, so it's hard to locate the tracts. And frequently the prices of the new homes are so high that it's scary.

The Early Bird Gets the Worm

Here's a story that is perfectly commonplace when the market heats up. I have a friend who wanted to buy a brand-new home in a suburb of San Francisco. This was at a time when the market was almost too hot to touch.

However, my friend was determined. Each day after work Jerry would cruise the neighborhood looking for signs of new construction—lots being bulldozed, houses being framed, even signs indicating that a builder was going to develop a tract on a certain piece of land.

Eventually Jerry located a tract he liked. It was the second phase of a builder's earlier development. When Jerry found it, the lots were just being bulldozed. No construction had started.

There really was no one there to talk to. So Jerry flagged down a bulldozer driver and asked where he could find the construction foreman. From that person he learned who the developer was and called the developer's office.

The developer told him that while she had plans for the houses being constructed, she hadn't yet finalized plans for their cost. She took his name and promised to call him back as soon as she had calculated how much the houses would sell for.

Jerry didn't take any chances. He called her every week for two months until finally she gave him a price list and indicated that the construction company would begin accepting offers to purchase on June 10, a month hence.

Jerry got a copy of the plans (the models weren't yet built) and went around to the building sites, deciding finally on a particular lot and design he preferred. The cost was $35,000 more than he thought he could afford; however, he borrowed from his parents in order to be sure he could buy the house.

Four days before the builder was going to accept offers, Jerry, complete with cot, sleeping bag, thermos, and ice chest filled with food, set up residence in front of the builder's office. Mind you, this was four days early.

Jerry was the first one there. However, within hours of his arrival, half a dozen other people showed up and camped out behind him. By the next day the line had swollen to over two dozen. Two days before the houses were to go on sale, there were more than 50 people in line. Keep in mind that only 28 houses were going to be sold.

To help keep things orderly, Jerry made a list of who was in line in what position and gave it to the developer, who agreed to honor it. Finally the fateful day arrived. Jerry was the first one in, the first to give his deposit, the first to sign a sales agreement. (There obviously was no haggling on price or terms—Jerry accepted whatever the builder dictated.) Then he went home to the first decent night's sleep in nearly a week.

It took six months to build the homes. Finally, after some harrowing troubles with qualifying for the lender (Jerry borrowed extra money from relatives), he got the house and moved in. His house came with no fences, no yard, and very few amenities inside. He paid more than he wanted to, but he was in.

Question: Was it a good move for Jerry?

Depends when you ask. Three months after Jerry moved in, he was offered a $55,000 profit if he would sell. He laughed and hung on. A year later the housing recession of the 1990s hit California and the value of his home plummeted. The price dropped by $50,000 more than he paid.

Jerry hung on and got caught in the housing boom at the turn of the century. Since then his house has gone up more than $150,000 over what he paid for it.

TIP—IT'S NOT HOW MUCH YOU PAY, IT'S WHEN YOU BUY AND SELL

Markets go both ways. Sometimes the most important thing is knowing when to take your profit and when to hang on.

Should You Buy a Not-Yet-Built Home?

You may have a choice between buying an already built brand new home or one that a builder has yet to put up. There are pros and cons with going each way.

With the already-built home, you know what you're getting and usually can see the neighborhood. But, with the yet-to-be-built home, items can be changed to fit your specific needs.

My suggestion is that whenever possible, always buy a home that is already built. I believe that knowing what you're going to get is more important than being able to customize a plan. Besides, you know for certain that it's actually going to get built.

What If the Builder is Slow or Stops Construction?

You can't make a builder go faster, or put up a home when he or she stops work. Usually, tardiness or a halt in construction is caused by circumstances beyond the builder's control, such as problems with financing, labor troubles, or problems with the local building department

---

The "Coming-Soon" Syndrome

Another friend of mine wanted to buy a new home in a development in Orange County, south of Los Angeles. Jill loved the location and fell in love with one of the models. There were several homes already constructed and ready for sale, but not the model she wanted. The builder told Jill that her model would be available in the "next phase." He took a $500 refundable deposit from her and signed an agreement, explaining that she would be required to fill out a sales agreement as soon as the house was built. The $500 merely reserved the house for her. He guessed that it would be ready in four months.

Four months later the builder hadn't even broken ground. Jill, and a number of others, were haunting his offices trying to find out what the problem was. All she could get were vague answers.

She was told that the lenders would not agree to the financing because of some title problems. Or there was a permit difficulty with the city. Or the builder was waiting until materials costs came down. Or something else.

Finally, five months after Jill paid her deposit, work began. It took another eight months to finish her home.

During the building period, she visited the home whenever she could, sometimes several visits a week. She didn't notice any problems until the house was almost completed and the wallboards put up. Then she realized that the floor plan was not exactly the same as the model. The windows of the living room didn't face the hills, the one feature she admired most about the plan.

She confronted the builder. Yes, he explained, the plans were changed. Building costs had changed and he was just adjusting to them. A few corners had been cut here and there so that he could deliver the property at the agreed-upon price. What could she do? She continued to wait.

Finally, the building was completed. It wasn't at all what Jill hoped it would be. But after all the waiting (nearly 11 months), she was glad she would be able to move in.

When she went to sign the sales agreement, however, she found that the price had gone up by $40,000! How could that be, she wanted to know? She had agreed upon a price with the builder. He pointed out that the price he agreed upon was the price of 11 months earlier. Costs had gone up since then, both building materials and labor. And housing prices had likewise increased. She didn't expect him to sell for yesterday's price, did she? He pointed to a clause in their agreement that clearly stated he could adjust the price.

In the end, it wasn't the house Jill wanted at the price she wanted to pay. She got her $500 deposit back and began to look elsewhere. However, she had lost nearly a year, not to mention all the hassle.

Yes, this is a true story. No, it doesn't happen all the time. It probably doesn't happen most of the time (although price and plan changes are legendary in construction). But it does happen enough that you should be aware of it and at least plan on the possibility.

Don't Forget the Upgrades

You'll quickly discover that when you buy a new home, there are plenty of upgrades available. Here's a list of some of the upgrades you can typically expect to pay more for:

Common Upgrades

- Larger or view lot
- Any changes in the basic construction plan
- Landscaped yard
- Better roof
- Better carpeting or tile
- Air conditioning (now standard on many homes)
- Additional mirrors or windows
- Better appliances (stove, oven, dishwasher, refrigerator)
- Better fixtures (toilets, sinks, tubs)
- Larger water heater

What's interesting is that while you may have your choice of a variety of upgrades, chances are you'll only be able to choose from the builder's list at the builder's price. For example, you may have your choice of three grades of carpet and that's it. Or you can choose from six tile patterns, three of which cost extra; no other changes may be allowed.

TRAP—DON'T EXPECT AN ALLOWANCE

So, you don't like what the builder offers? And chances are you don't like the upgrade prices? So what do you do? The most logical thing is to tell the builder no thanks and that you'd like an allowance for his cost of materials. You'll go out and buy your own. Not a chance (in most cases)! Most builders will *not* give you an allowance against standard items.

There are several reasons that builders limit the changes and upgrades you can make. One is cost. They get guaranteed estimates from a few distributors and they know what it's going to cost to purchase a particular product. That makes it easy for them to stick with that product.

Also, there's the cost of labor as well as materials. Some materials require extra labor costs. For example, some Mexican tiles are irregular (when compared with American or European tiles), and there may be an extra labor charge for installing them. To avoid hassles here, the builder may simply limit the selection to half a dozen patterns, all because he knows he can control the labor costs.

Finally, there's the matter of lender and building department approval. The builder usually has lenders who have guaranteed approval of financing, provided the house is built a certain way with certain features. Change the features and a new appraisal might be necessary. Similarly, the plans may call for specific features. Change those features and the builder may have to submit new plans to the building department.

TRAP—MUST HAVE CARPETS

 Did you know that many building departments will not give final approval to a home until all the carpeting, appliances, and fixtures are in? Thus, even if you want to buy your own carpeting, for example, the builder can't agree to it and still "final" the home.

The real question you should ask yourself is: Which upgrades and extras are worthwhile and which are not? Here are some clues.

Is a Larger or View Lot Worth it?

If the price isn't that much more, go for it. For example, a lot with a view or a larger lot may cost 3 percent more than a standard lot. Usually this will pay in the long run. On the other hand, back off if the price is excessive. Keep in mind that if you buy a view lot, it may be the best money you can spend. If you're in an area where view lots are prized, you could get it back several times over when you sell.

On the other hand, beware if you buy a larger lot. Unless you landscape it so that it requires little to no maintenance work, it could be a drawback when you resell.

Is It Worthwhile to Upgrade Carpets and Floor Coverings?

Usually new homes come with wall-to-wall carpet, tile, and/or finished wood. But the quality of these often leaves much to be desired. The difference is most obvious with carpets and tiles. The model home may have luxurious, thick carpeting, whereas the actual carpeting that comes with your home may be short and skimpy. The model may have colorful Italian tiles while the standard home comes with ordinary white tiles.

I've found that it usually doesn't pay to upgrade floor coverings IF the builder is charging a hefty price for the privilege. In too many cases you can go out and buy the same upgraded floor covering for a fraction of the builder's price. Better to just live with the standard grade and then, after a year or two, replace it.

On the other hand, if money is no object and you want better floors, go for it!

Should I Pay for an Upgraded Yard?

Many homes these days come with a landscaped front yard. Almost none come with landscaped side and back yards. However, your builder will usually put these in for you, for a price.

This is usually an expensive trap. Putting in yards can be very costly. On the other hand, if you do some of the work yourself and hire out only the difficult tasks like installing the watering system and planting large trees, you can do it for significantly less.

Should I Upgrade to Air Conditioning?

Most new houses in the southern part of the country offer this as standard. If air conditioning is offered as an upgrade (instead of a standard feature), I would get it. The climate appears to be growing warmer in most parts of the country. Today, just as in automobiles, air conditioning is considered to be a necessary feature. You may find that you have trouble selling your house later on if it doesn't have air conditioning.

What About Other Upgrades?

It all depends on what they cost, how much better they make the house look, and how much more livability they add. My own rule-of-thumb is to go for upgrades whenever they are inexpensive and leave them off whenever the price is exorbitant.

How Can I Watch Out for Shoddy Construction?

One of the advantages of buying a resale is that you pretty well know what you're getting. If the home has been standing for 5, 10, or more years, chances are it will stand another 30 or 40.

On the other hand, when you purchase a new home, you're buying something that is as yet untried. If there are defects, they could show up in the first few years of usage.

But, I hear many readers saying, aren't new homes fully inspected by city or county building departments? Don't they have to meet strict health and safety guidelines?

Yes . . . and no. All modern buildings are inspected at numerous times during their construction. In most cases, the inspector catches problems and forces their correction before a "certificate of occupancy" is granted. (You can't occupy the home without this certificate—in most areas you can't even connect to water, power, or gas without it.)

However, there may be only one or two building inspectors and hundreds of houses to inspect. Further, while in most cases the inspectors are well trained and experienced, they often are not expert in every area of construction. And in a few cases they simply are not very well qualified.

The upshot of all this is that regardless of the area of the country, shoddy construction goes on all the time right next to excellent construction. For example, a few years ago the builder of a housing tract in Southern California decided to use a Spanish tile roof. This consists of red, curved tiles interlaced to form a very attractive roofline.

The trouble with the tiles is that they aren't very good at holding out water. In a wind-driven storm, the water sweeps up under the edges of the tiles and through the roofs. In the old days (the 1700s), Spanish tile roofs were used extensively in California. However, in those days a kind of mortar was applied to the roof and the tiles were carefully set into it. This effectively waterproofed them.

Today the use of this mortar would be unattractive and expensive. So instead, roofers lay down layers of heavy, waterproof tar paper called "felt" before placing the tiles. It acts as an effective water barrier.

However, in this particular tract the roofer had never before laid Spanish tiles. No felt was placed beneath them. The building inspector, also unfamiliar with the need for felt, didn't catch it.

You're right. With the first rain the roofs leaked—every roof in a tract of over 60 houses! About two-thirds had been sold and the water damage forced the occupants out. Needless to say, they were furious and everyone looked to the builder for repairs. The builder was an honorable person, but not particularly wealthy. All the tiles on the roofs had to be removed and felt placed underneath. It meant reroofing over 60 homes—a very, very costly thing to do. The builder simply couldn't handle it and declared bankruptcy.

Note, this was shoddy construction. But no one was really trying to cut corners. It was just a case of a builder working in an area of unfamiliarity and a building inspector likewise being in the dark

Of course, this is a dramatic exception. Most buyers of new homes have no problems at all (or small problems which the builder quickly fixes). But that doesn't mean that major structural problems in workmanship or even materials couldn't occur. In a way it's like buying a car. Chances are the one you get will be wonderful. On the other hand, you could get a lemon. All of which is a great recommendation for getting your building thoroughly inspected (during construction, if possible) by a professional inspector (see Chapter 15).

What About Builder Warranities?

Most builders back their construction with warranties. Even a builder who does not give you a written warranty may be offering you an "implied" warranty, depending upon the state in which you live. Today many states have strong consumer protection laws that allow you to take the builder to court for shoddy construction and win a settlement. (Of course, that's of dubious value if the builder has gone broke.) Often the warranties run for 10 years or more, although specific types of repairs or replacements may be limited to only 1 year.

Of that vast majority of builders who offer warranties, there are two groups: Those who self-warrant and those who buy insurance.

Self-Warranted Homes

A builder who self-warrants a home will normally give you a certificate of warranty, which states what is covered and what is not covered. Typically such a warranty says that if it's not specifically noted, it's not covered.

The Magnuson-Moss Act (1975) is a disclosure law that is handled by the Federal Trade Commission (FTC). Under Magnuson-Moss, you may be entitled to specific protections. They should include the following:

What to Look For in a Builder's Warranty

- The name of the person who is warranted (you) and a specific statement of whether the warranty is transferable if you sell the property.
- Precise information on what is covered and what is excluded.
- Exact language detailing what a builder will do to correct a problem that arises.
- The length of the warranty.
- The procedure, in detail, for filing a claim.
- Any limitations on consequential damages. (Consequential damages result as a consequence of covered problems. The most common example is a water pipe bursting, causing damage to furniture. The pipe may be covered, but is the furniture?)
- A clear statement of any reduction of implied warranties.

TRAP—DON'T WAIVE YOUR RIGHTS

 As part of the warranty, some builders have the buyers sign a statement that they waive all implied warranties. In the states that permit this, if you sign such a statement, you may give up more rights than you get, since the implied warranties may be stronger than the builder's specific warranties. If a builder insists you sign a waiver statement, you may want to consider a different builder and house. At least check it over with your attorney.

Under a builder's warranty, you have to go back to the builder to get satisfaction if a problem arises. It's to your advantage, therefore, to find a builder who is big enough to sustain the losses involved with any likely problems.

Insurance-Warranted Homes

A different kind of warranty is offered by a large group of builders nationwide. This is a warranty backed not only by the builder but also by an insurance company. Typically under these policies the builder continues to warrant the house, but the insurance company backs up that warranty. In addition, it often offers a plan that changes with the years the house is in existence, offering greater protection in the first years and less in the later ones.

Many insurance-backed warranties are transferable. However, there may be limitations and exclusions. Usually under these plans, your first recourse is to seek a solution to the problem from the builder. If the builder does not or is not able to comply, the insurance company picks up the tab for covered items after a deductible is paid.

Should I Get a Home Inspection?

Yes, as noted above. Just because it's a new home, that doesn't mean it's built right. You should have it inspected both before you move in, and if possible, several times during the construction phase. A good builder will not only allow you to do this, but will encourage you to do it.

A professional home inspector (see Chapter 15 on finding one) should be able to give you all sorts of help here. You'll want someone with strong construction background who can check everything from the pouring of the foundation to electrical, plumbing, roofing, drywall, and finishing.

Don't make the mistake of confusing "new" with "good." Yes, it may be good work . . . but then, again, it just might not be.

How Do I Find a Good Builder?

Most of us simply shop houses. We go from tract to tract trying to find the new home that will be just right for us. It's also important, however, to shop builders. As should be evident from the discussions on shoddy workmanship and on warranties, a lot depends on the builder. You want a builder who does good work and who has the means to back it up should any unforeseen problems arise.

Here's a checklist to help determine the quality of the builder:

Checklist for Selecting a Good Builder

- How long has the builder been constructing new homes? (Longevity is always a good sign.)
- Can you get a recommendation (or a condemnation!) from a relative, friend, or associate who's previously had dealings with the builder?
- Check with the Better Business Bureau. This organization normally keeps complaints filed against businesses. Does the builder have many complaints filed?
- Check with any consumer groups active in the area. Also check with the local office of the National Association of Home Builders. Your builder may be a member of this group and it may be able to give a recommendation.
- Find out where the builder has previously built new homes. Go to the tract and knock on a few doors. Simply say you are going to be buying a home from the same builder and you would like to know if those who bought

before had any difficulties, such as shoddy work or reluctance to fix problems. Don't be embarrassed. Homeowners love to talk about their builder. Either she's wonderful and has done a marvelous job. Or he's been a disaster for them. Just be sure you talk to more than one person to get a balanced viewpoint.

Can I Negotiate Price with the Builder?

Now we come to the tricky part for many new home buyers: negotiating with the builder. Here many who purchase a new home are completely lost, signing anything and everything that is placed before them.

Just as with purchasing a resale, when buying a new home everything is negotiable. The problem with new homes, however, is that the builder is often tied into financing and labor and materials contracts so that he or she cannot really offer the flexibility that an owner of a resale can.

Typically when buying a new home, you are presented with a colorful and expensive-looking brochure that gives the floor plans of the various models that the builder is offering. Along with these is usually a price schedule. For Plan A the price is $185,000 until January 2, when the price goes up to $187,500. For Plan B the price is $235,000. For Plan C it's $268,000. And so forth.

In addition, there are premiums for better lots as well as additional costs for upgrades, as described earlier. Thus the prices are laid out in the same fashion as they are in a grocery store. You certainly can't bargain with the grocer over the price of a jar of mayonnaise. How do you bargain with a builder over the price list for a new home?

TRAP—DON'T GET SUCKERED

It's important to understand that builders and developers like to create the impression that nothing is negotiable—either you take their price or you don't get the house. That's part of the reason for the elaborate brochures. The truth, however, is that builders are real estate sellers just like any other. When builders need to get rid of homes, they will negotiate down to the bare bones, regardless of what the brochures say.

The way you negotiate with builders is to say that you would "like to submit an offer on one of the houses." The tract salesperson should be a licensed real estate agent and he or she, acting as a fiduciary for the builder, should submit all offers (unless the builder has stipulated in writing that no offers be submitted below a specific price—an unlikely possibility). A better way is to have a buyer's agent do the negotiating for you. However, here you could be liable for a commission.

The easiest way to negotiate is to find a builder who already has houses up. This builder is paying a hefty finance charge each month that the houses remain unsold. This builder is highly motivated to sell the property.

However, as noted, builders may not have a lot of wiggle room with regard to price. They usually have enormous flexibility, however, when it comes to upgrades.

Yes, you'll pay their price, but you want an upgrade of carpet at no additional cost to you, and you want a self-cleaning oven instead of the standard oven included with the home, and you want floor-to-ceiling mirrors in the bathrooms, and so on.

Remember, the builder gets the upgrades wholesale. If he or she simply passes them on to you at cost, it probably won't be a hardship to the builder. And it could save you thousands.

On the other hand, don't expect the builder to budge when the market's hot or when the houses haven't yet been constructed. In this case, there's no leverage on your side. Why should the builder accept a lower offer when there are other buyers willing to pay full price or when the builder hasn't even put up the houses and isn't paying interest on them?

Don't Forget to Bargain on Terms

This is often the case when interest rates are higher and it's difficult for buyers to qualify for mortgages.

The builder may be willing to "pay down" the mortgage by several points. For example, you'll get the mortgage. However, instead of paying the going rate of, say, 9 percent for the first 3 years, you might pay 7 percent, with the builder paying the other 2 percent.

On a $200,000 mortgage, 2 percentage points can save you roughly $4000 a year in interest payments.

But beware of builders who pay down the mortgage just to raise the price by an offsetting amount. In the above example, you would save close to $6000 over a three-year buy down. But if the builder raised the price of the property by $6000, where would your savings be? You'd be converting a lower payment into a higher price. And after the first three years, you'd be paying mortgage interest on that higher price.

In most cases, a builder won't buy down an interest rate unless the houses have been sitting around for awhile and interest rates are keeping buyers away.

TIP—CHECK FOR THE ORIGINAL PRICE

By talking to those who bought six months ago in the same tract, you should be able to establish what the original pricing was. Thus you can determine if the builder has raised the price to pay for your buy down.

13

Buying Directly from Sellers (FSBOs) and Saving

"FSBO" is an acronym for "For Sale by Owner." There are always some FSBOs available in any neighborhood. When the market is hot and houses are selling well, sellers try to avoid paying a commission by selling themselves. When the market is cold and houses aren't selling, sellers eventually give up on agents and try to sell by themselves.

If you're house hunting, you owe it to yourself to check out the FSBOs in the area where you want to live. You just might find exactly what you're looking for. When you do drop by (usually it's best to call first, since many sellers working without agents are wary of strangers), expect to be courteously shown around the property.

Take the time to check out the home. Look it over carefully, especially since you won't have an agent along to point out good parts . . . and bad.

If you decide that you really like it, then the real work starts—dealing with the sellers direct. Unfortunately, many FSBO sellers have only a vague idea of what the market price for their house should be. Most often they are asking too much. If you suggest this to them, they may be insulted. It is very difficult to negotiate terms or price reductions with them because of the one-on-one relationship between you, the buyer, and the seller. Unless you're well versed in real estate, you'll probably find it's difficult to deal with FSBO sellers. Additionally, there's the matter of resolving how the paperwork will be handled. We cover resolving these issues in this chapter.

163

TIP—HAVE A BUYER'S AGENT
HELP YOU OUT

 One way of handling FSBOs is to work with a "buyer's agent." Prearrange with the agent. (See Chapter 6 for tips on how this is done.) When you find an FSBO that you like, the agent will step in and handle the negotiations. Of course, for his role, the agent will expect at least a buyer's agent's commission (usually half of a full commission). Often agents can convince the sellers to pay this. But if that's not possible, you could be on the hook for it! Be sure you determine in advance how your buyer's agent will handle commissions.

My own experience with FSBOs has been mixed. As a buyer, I have walked the streets stopping at FSBOs and talking to sellers. I have tried to buy the homes for myself. Unless the seller is just trying to sell by owner for a few weeks before listing, the results have almost universally been dismal. Typically a determined FSBO seller wants too much for the property or is inflexible when it comes to the terms. In other words, I can usually make a better deal on a property that is listed by an agent. But not always.

Why Does a Seller Go FSBO?

Almost 90 percent of sellers who start out trying to sell FSBO eventually give up and sell using an agent. Why don't they simply list to begin with and save time?

The answer is that they want to save money. They're hoping that you (or some buyer) will come along and pay them full price, take care of the financing, and let them avoid paying the big 6 (or 5, or 7, or whatever) percent commission to the agent.

What few FSBOs recognize is that what's important is selling the home. And trying to get an unrealistic price is wasting the seller's time. It's wasting your time, too.

However, every once in awhile, you'll come across an FSBO who really wants to sell quickly and understands that by giving you a bargain price, he or she can not only save a little on the commission, but also get a quicker sale. That's the FSBO you're trying to find.

TRAP—YOU SHOULD PAY LESS FOR A FSBO?

Remember, you're not getting the benefit of an agent oiling the waters to make the deal go smoothly. You have to do some of the work, or hire an attorney or agent to do it for you. Therefore, there's every reason to expect to pay *less* for a FSBO.

Where Do I Find FSBOs?

Walk neighborhoods where you want to live and buy a home. Drive the streets. Look for signs that say the house is for sale by owner.

Also check for "assisted" sale home. Some brokerage agencies, such as "Assist-to-Sell" will provide signs and some assistance to sellers who are trying to sell by themselves.

Try checking the local newspapers under the head, "For Sale by Owner." Sometimes there will be many ads there, sometimes only a few. If any are in your price range and where you want to buy, call them right up and get out there to look at the property.

And check the Internet. There are dozens, sometimes hundreds, of FSBO sites. I'm not listing any FSBO sites here simply because they seem to come and go with surprising frequency. Just use a good search engine to locate them. (Key in the words "FSBO" or "by owner real estate."

Don't be hesitant to check out any properties you find on the Internet. Usually the seller's name and phone is given. Just call him or her and continue on as if you had seen the ad in the paper. But remember that the Internet is worldwide. Be sure that a property you find is, in fact, in a location where you want to buy. It could be in the next town, or the next continent!

Do I Just Walk In and Say Hello?

Unlike when you're touring with an agent, when you can wear whatever you want and act anyway you like, when you first meet a FSBO, you should be on best behavior.

Dress well. Be polite. Don't hog the conversation. Let the FSBO give you a tour of the property. Add the complimentary "oohs" and "aahs" at the usual places. In other words, try to make a good impression. Remember, if it turns out that this is the place you want to buy, this seller is the person with whom you're going to negotiate and with whom you're going to take the sale journey.

If you like the place, I recommend that you don't begin negotiations on your first visit. Rather, use that as strictly an exploratory mission. Try to find out as much about the property and the seller's motivation as you can. At the same time the seller will be trying to assess you and your intentions.

Later, after you've left and had a chance to think about it, if you still like the place, call the seller and arrange another time to come down and negotiate. Waiting has the added effect of letting the seller know you're not too anxious. And calling for an appointment allows the seller to build anticipation as to what you might have on your mind, how much you might offer. It gets the seller more interested in seeing what you've got.

TRAP—DON'T BE IN A HURRY

Don't plan on simply breezing in, making an offer, and then breezing out. Plan to spend time, hours if necessary. Use "small talk." Get to know the sellers better. Let them get to know you. When you present your offer, present it one element at a time. Sometimes, if you're lowballing, it's better to present the favorable terms first with the price last. The more time you and the seller spend together, the more likely you are both to be committed to working out a deal. After all, no one likes to "waste" an entire evening with nothing to show for it. After awhile, the seller will begin bending over backwards to "save" the deal.

Finding the Enlightened FSBO

Let's say you've dropped in on half a dozen FSBOs and realized that they either weren't for you, or if you liked them, the prices were too high for the market. Now, suddenly, you find an FSBO in the neighborhood and discover the seller is enlightened. He tells you that homes like his in the area go for $300,000. However, he's selling by owner and realizes that's a harder sell. So he'll cut the price by an amount equal to half a commission, $9000 in a price reduction, if you'll buy directly. The price will be $291,000.

Right off the top you're offered half the value of the commission in a price reduction. Now it's a matter of negotiation. You point out that, yes, you're willing to buy. But since there's no agent, you've got to do all the usual work that the broker performs. Plus, you've got the risks of dealing directly with a seller. You want a price reduction equal to the full commission.

The FSBO balks, and maybe you compromise somewhere in between. Or maybe he agrees. Remember, he's keeping his eye on the doughnut and not the hole. He wants the sale.

If all goes well, you've just gotten the home at a lesser price.

How Do You Handle Paperwork in an FSBO Deal?

The correct answer is, "Very carefully!"

You can't trust an inexperienced seller, one who probably lacks the knowledge to handle the paperwork for the transaction. This is an area that tolerates few mistakes. The wrong language, a misinterpretation of a law, the failure to include some important item such as your demand for a professional home inspection, could result in a bad deal that could hurt you or that might end up in litigation. You want it done right.

In actuality an enlightened FSBO will already have considered this problem and come up with a viable solution. That solution, usually, is to have an agent prepare the purchase agreement and other paperwork on a fee-for-service basis. Alternatively, the seller may be having an attorney do it.

TIP—THE BEST ATTORNEY PRICE IN TOWN

On the East Coast, the usual price for having a real estate attorney handle all the paperwork in a typical transaction is between $750 and $1500 (depending on what's involved). Today the many new fee-for-service agents charge similar amounts (see Chapter 6). Keep in mind, however, that while attorneys that handle real estate transactions are found all over the East Coast, they are seldom found in other parts of the country. Fee-for-service agents, however, are cropping up everywhere.

If the seller hasn't come up with this solution, you can come up with it yourself. Just be sure that you agree in advance who will pay the costs of having the paperwork done.

What About Arranging for Inspections and Getting Repairs Done?

That's what the agent does. No agent? Then it's up to you or the seller. It's a good idea to get an initial understanding between yourself and the seller on the delegation of responsibilities. The last thing you want is to think that the seller is doing something while, in reality, he or she thinks you're handling it.

Your fee-for-service agent, your attorney, or your escrow officer can come up with a good list of things that need to be done in order to close escrow. Then delegate who will do what. But be sure to call the seller occasionally to see that he or she is doing her part. You don't want to come to the end of escrow only to discover that the seller hasn't even started with termite repair work.

Can I Negotiate with a FSBO Seller?

Yes, but usually with difficulty. Face-to-face negotiations are something that most of us cringe at. Yet, to get a home at a better price by buying from a FSBO, it's something we'll have to do. Here are some helpful points to remember:

FSBO Negotiating Tactics

- Remember, this is business. Never say anything personally disparaging to the seller. To do so will almost immediately end the negotiations. If the seller says something personal against you, make note of it, and then move on. If you hold it personally against the seller, again the deal's likely to come unraveled.

- Argue at your peril. Always remember that if you argue with the seller, there's no third party to settle the argument. You could each end up in a rigid, uncompromising position that would make consummating a deal impossible. Instead, simply listen to the seller and then present your position. If you're at odds, then look for common ground and whittle away until you're both in agreement. Sound easier than it is? Perhaps, but with a little practice and keeping a cool head, it works surprisingly well.

- Never lie, not even a tiny, little small one. If you have a credit problem, you don't necessarily have to bring it up. (Although if it's going to affect the deal, getting it out in the open early on is a good idea.) However, once it comes up, don't lie about it. Don't make it bigger than it is, but don't make it smaller either. Lies, even small ones, have a way of poisoning the negotiation. If the seller catches you in a lie, he or she begins wondering what else you're lying about. Maybe you're just there to cheat the seller? Maybe you really don't have the cash to buy or can't qualify for the mortgage. And on and on. Telling the truth may hurt, but it hurts a lot less than lying.

- When the sellers' price is way off, let them know. But back your comments up with facts. Have a list of recent comparable sales in the area to point to. Let the facts do the work for you. Figures don't lie. They tell what the house is worth.

Get It in Writing

You may be agreed on Monday morning. But by Thursday morning the sellers may be having second thoughts and want to start negotiations all over again.

Get yourself immediately down to an attorney or agent who'll write up the deal, and then get everyone's signature. Only then can you breathe a conditional sigh of relief (conditioned on the deal finally closing some 30 days later after you get financing, the seller clears title, and everything goes according to plan).

14
Buying a Lot, Building a Home Yourself, and Saving

Why buy someone else's home when you can design and build your own?

You'd certainly be the rare person if the thought hadn't at least crossed your mind at some point in your life. It's the secret dream of a great many of us. I know it was the dream of my wife and myself when we first did it years ago in the Sierra woods of Northern California. The lessons we learned, as well as those of other self-builders with whom I've talked, can be extremely helpful if you're starting to think more seriously about this.

TIP—BUT CAN I REALLY DO IT?

You probably can. It doesn't take as much money as you might think. It doesn't take as much specialized knowledge. What it does take is a lot of time and determination.

TRAP—BUT WILL I DO A GOOD JOB?

 Chances are you can't do it better than builders whose profession is putting up homes. They know materials and labor, design and construction, as well as where to cut corners and where to be lavish. But what you can offer that they can't is your own unique approach.

I firmly believe that everyone should build their own home at least once. It's an experience you'll cherish and never forget. And the home you produce will always have a warm spot in your heart.

Start with the Lot

The first thing you must do is find a lot. These days most people who construct their own homes do so in rural or vacation areas (developers having already built up most suburban areas). Lots are for sale everywhere, but good lots are hard to find. Here's a checklist of what to look for in a good lot:

Lot Checklist

Location

Everyone knows that location is important in real estate, but it is doubly important in rural or vacation areas. The reason is simple. Properties here can take much longer to sell (frequently years). If you want to resell, you're going to need a prime location so you can get out relatively quickly. Does your lot have the following (in order of importance)?

	YES	NO
■ Water Frontage (river or lake)?	[ ]	[ ]
■ View?	[ ]	[ ]
■ Level building site?	[ ]	[ ]
■ Easy access roads?	[ ]	[ ]
■ Close to urban/suburban area?	[ ]	[ ]

Lot Amenities

These are the features of the particular lot that you find. Some lots are grand, while others are not so grand. Does yours have:

- Lots of trees?   [ ] [ ]
- A lot of room? (Sometimes a minus in the city, but usually a plus in the country.)   [ ] [ ]
- Good building soil? (It's harder to build in a swamp or "rock country.")   [ ] [ ]
- A lot of level ground? (It's also harder to build on a mountainside.)   [ ] [ ]

Water

In the city it's something we take for granted, but building in the country, it's a prime consideration. Does your lot have:

- A well? (Not so good, but better than no water!)   [ ] [ ]
- A mutual or private water company (Good)   [ ] [ ]
- Water for irrigation? (Gardening)   [ ] [ ]

Sewer System

It's something important to consider before you buy. Does your lot:

- Have access to a public a sewer system? (How much will it cost you to hook up to it?)   [ ] [ ]
- Require a septic tank? (Do you have enough room for a leach field?)   [ ] [ ]

Power

Yes, many rural or mountain lots have not yet been accessed by the power company. It's a very big negative.

- Does your lot have electric power?   [ ] [ ]
- If not, is it coming soon?   [ ] [ ]

Drainage

This can be a big factor later on, although it's something few of us remember to consider when we buy.

- Does your lot drain adequately?   [ ] [ ]
- Are there soft, wet areas indicating heavy water buildup?   [ ] [ ]
- Will you need to dig drainage ditches before you build?   [ ] [ ]

Title

Buying a lot is not quite the same as buying a house. You have to worry about all kinds of restrictions.

- Can you get clear title?   [ ] [ ]
- Are there any easements (to power companies, water companies, and so on) on your lot?   [ ] [ ]

- Are those easements just where you want to build? (If they
  are, you won't be able to.)   [ ]   [ ]
- Are you in any kind of restricted area that would impair
  your ability to build:
  - a coastal preserve?   [ ]   [ ]
  - a national forest?   [ ]   [ ]
  - a wildlife preserve?   [ ]   [ ]
  - other?   [ ]   [ ]
  - Is there a building moratorium in your area?   [ ]   [ ]

Environmental Concerns

These are important issues that you usually have to dig to discover:

- Is your area facing any kind of environmental impact
  control?   [ ]   [ ]
- Is there something occurring in the area that would severely
  affect the value of your property?
  - draining a lake?   [ ]   [ ]
  - changing the course of a river?   [ ]   [ ]
  - lumbering activity?   [ ]   [ ]
  - Is your lot located in a geologically unstable area
    (earthquakes)?   [ ]   [ ]
  - Anything else that's detrimental   [ ]   [ ]

Watch Out for Those Leach Fields

"Leach fields" are something new to many first-time home builders
in rural areas. If you have a septic system, it is composed of two ele-
ments: the tank, which holds the solid sewerage, and the leach field,
which drains out the liquid sewerage. A tank takes up only a few
dozen square feet. A leach field, on the other hand, requires hundreds of square feet, usually in a flat area. Be sure you have enough
room for your leach field as well as your building site when looking
at a rural lot. Have the county sanitation engineer check it out.

Watch Out for Wells and Puddles

Beware of lots that have their own wells. Chances are you'll be
required to put in a septic tank for sewerage. Unless the lot is very

large, the septic leach field may interfere with the well water. In short, it may be difficult to secure a building permit, and even if you do you stand the chance of poisoning yourself.

Also, many buyers look at their future lot in only one season. In the fall, for example, the lot may be dry and covered with beautiful foliage. However, in the spring, it may be a swamp from stagnant winter rain runoff.

Be sure to talk to local residents to get a picture of what your lot is going to be like all year long. Also look for ditches that neighbors have dug as well as natural water runoffs—these indicate the drainage of the lot. Beware of flat areas with no runoff, as they could become pools of water (or ice) in other seasons.

Watch Out for Poor Soil Quality

The quality of soil is a crucial factor when building. Ideally, you want soil that allows water to percolate yet retains its shape. Expansive soils (mostly clays) expand when they get wet, and this can easily lead to cracked foundations. Sandy soils can more easily wash away. If there is any doubt at all, get a soils report from a qualified engineering company.

How Are Lots Financed?

Generally, lots are paid for either in cash or with a mortgage carried back by the seller (typically for a term of under 10 years at prevailing interest rates). It would be a mistake to buy a lot thinking you can refinance it through a bank or savings and loan. Most lenders won't loan on bare land. Banks, when they will loan, generally will give only 50 percent or less of the appraised value.

TIP—GET THE SELLER TO CARRY PAPER

Don't be hesitant to make a bold offer on financing a lot. For example, you may offer 10 percent down with the owners to carry a mortgage for the balance over 10

years at 2 percent below the current interest rate. Remember that lots are hard to sell and that frequently people own them free and clear. You're not going to get such a favorable (to you) offer accepted every time, but you will get it accepted more often than you might think.

What About Construction Plans?

Once you have your lot, the next step is to get a set of construction plans. This can be a very expensive or a very inexpensive task. At one end are the ready-made plans that are available through the mail from building magazines (just check your newsstands). At the other end of the spectrum, you can hire an architect to draw up a set of plans just for you.

Mail-Order Plans

Mail order is definitely the cheapest way to go, since a set of plans can be obtained for just a few hundred dollars. There are literally thousands of mail-order plans available. Be sure you check to see that they are appropriate for your area of the country and that the building materials list doesn't involve some overly expensive timbers or metal.

Be careful, however, if you buy through-the-mail plans. A "working set" includes all elevations as well as details of all unusual construction. Some of the plans that I have seen sent through the mail are simply a front view and an inside view. They definitely give you enough to see what the house will look like, but they're a far cry from being detailed enough for you or a builder to work with. If you order through the mail, be sure that there is a full "money back" guarantee. In addition, as soon as you get the plans, take them to a builder to see if they are adequate. Expect to pay around $500 for a set of mail-order plans.

TIP—GET THEM CUSTOMIZED

Even if you order plans through the mail, you will probably have to modify them to accommodate your building site. Why not hire a local architect on an hourly basis to modify these plans? The cost can be a fraction of what drawing up a set of plans from scratch would be.

Custom-Made Plans

Custom-made is the most expensive way to go, but you can arrive at a unique and well-built house. You hire an architect to draft a set of plans for you. Typically, the cost is 3 to 5 percent of the cost of building the house. (If it costs $100,000 to build the house, figure $3000 to $5000 for the plans.)

A good architect will visit the building site and design the plans to fit the contour of the land. In addition, the architect will listen carefully to your desires for a home and incorporate those features that you want.

Finally, a good architect will be aware of building codes and building materials costs in your area and will design a house to take advantage of whatever cost savings are possible.

Interview the architect as you would any other person you are hiring. Ask to see plans that the architect has previously done. (Sometimes you can save money by modifying an existing set of plans.) Find out who the architect has designed houses for and then call up those owners. Did they like the work? Did the architect take advantage of cost savings wherever possible? Would the owners recommend the person?

Find out first what the costs will be. Some architects work on an hourly basis; others have a set fee. Don't assume that the costs will be minimal. Plans can be very expensive.

Do-It-Yourself Plans

In most areas of the country if you agree to live on the property for at least a year, you are permitted not only to do all or most of the construction yourself but also to draw up the plans. No, this is not an impossible task. I've done it myself and I have no background in architecture or drafting. What I did was to study the lot and then design a house that took advantage of the view. I then hired a draftsperson to create a set of working construction plans on the basis of my rough sketches.

Finally I hired an engineer to determine the required loads. The total cost to me was under $1500. You can do it, too.

Consult with the Building Department

Work with your local building department, not against it. Find out in advance what special requirements it has (snow load, wind resistance, insulation, sewer systems, and so on). Incorporate these features into your plans at an early stage. Get to know your local building inspectors and ask for advice. They may save you hours of time and thousands of dollars by suggesting approved methods of building that you may not have thought of.

How Do I Find a Good Builder?

Of course, you can build it all yourself, if you happen to be a relative of Hercules. However, some of the work is extremely hard, such as pouring concrete and lifting heavy timbers. Some requires special skills, such as soldering, plumbing, and plastering. And some is just plain tedious, such as putting up siding and sheet rock.

The alternative is to hire workpeople and/or a builder. Unless you plan to do at least 75 percent of the work yourself, you're better off striking a deal with a builder. Keep in mind, however, that many builders are interested only in making a set profit on each job. When you submit a set of plans to them for a bid, they simply add up the square footage, multiply by a predetermined price, and that's your cost. You might be better off with a builder who looks closely at the plans and figures the actual costs.

If you plan to do some of the work—finish the house, for example—you need to find a builder who actually does true cost estimates. These include finding out what the materials and labor will actually cost and then calculating profit on top of that. In a house I built a few years ago, two builders went the first route, bidding by square footage. The third builder took the other course. The third builder's price was 30 percent lower than that of the first two because he looked closely at actual costs of labor and materials!

TIP—BE YOUR OWN CONTRACTOR

If you do most of the work yourself, you can hire workpeople to do the remaining chores for you. You can do, essentially, what the builder does. You can hire carpenters, plumbers, roofers, tapers, and so forth. However, those you hire typically work on a "per job" basis instead of an hourly basis. They will want to see your plans and then will "bid the job." If they see you're inexperienced, they may give you a high bid. To avoid this, be sure that you get at least three bids for each job.

Builder's Qualification Checklist

	YES	NO
■ Has your builder been in the business in the area of your lot for at least three years?	[ ]	[ ]
■ Is your builder state licensed?	[ ]	[ ]
■ Have you called the state licensing bureau to see if there are any complaints against your builder?	[ ]	[ ]
■ Have you called the local better business bureau or district attorney's office to see if there are complaints?	[ ]	[ ]
■ Have you visited other houses your builder has constructed?	[ ]	[ ]
■ Did the prior construction look solid?	[ ]	[ ]
■ Did the owners voice any complaints?	[ ]	[ ]
■ Did you call the local building supply company to ask if your builder was ever late making payments?	[ ]	[ ]
■ Is your builder ready and able to get started?	[ ]	[ ]
■ Do you get along well with your builder?	[ ]	[ ]

TRAP—BEWARE OF HOW YOU PAY AND TO WHOM

Most builders will want you to sign a building agreement in which you agree to provide them a series of payments out of which they will pay their workers and their materials suppliers. However, if you pay the builder and the builder does not pay the workers and suppliers, you could still be liable for full payment to those workers and suppliers. (They could file mechanic's liens on your property and force payment, even if you have to pay twice!) Your only recourse, in such an event, may be to sue the builder, who may have filed for bankruptcy. You can protect yourself by asking your builder to supply you with a completion bond. Most builders balk at this, however, because such bonds tend to be expensive and difficult to qualify for.

If you are securing financing in order to build, generally the lender will check out the builder and will withhold payments until the builder supplies proof of payment for labor and supplies. You can demand this proof (in the form of mechanic's "releases") too.

Again, however, it's a hassle for the builder, and many don't like doing it. In addition, sometimes the mechanics will give releases and then still file liens later on saying that the release was given on the builder's check, and the lien was filed when that check bounced!

Probably greater protection comes from insisting on paying subcontractors and materials suppliers yourself. The builder submits a "chit" or authorization, and you issue the check.

Again, however, builders don't like doing this because it allows you to see exactly how much they are paying for labor and materials and how much profit they are making on your house. Also, it tends to undermine their authority with the subcontractors.

TRAP—WATCH OUT FOR MECHANIC'S LIENS

 Be sure you understand mechanic's lien laws in your state. Check with a local contractor or, better still, an attorney to get the details.

Be There

You've bought the lot, had the plans drawn up, secured a builder (or hired subcontractors), and are ready to go. Once construction starts, plan on being there a great deal of the time or on having a builder or someone knowledgeable there to handle things.

There are always questions that pop up. What does that little squiggle on the plans mean? The plans call for a 3-foot foundation, but there's a 7-foot hole in the building site—what do we do?

Where do you want the electrical switches? And on and on. Somebody has to be there to handle the questions.

TRAP—DON'T COUNT ON THE INSPECTORS

 Don't count on the local building inspector to ensure that everything is done right. Building inspectors can't watch everything all the time. If you don't know how it should be built, hire someone who does to supervise the job. Plan on spending more time than you first estimate.

Workers don't show up on time. Building materials are delayed getting to the site. The weather turns against you. To be perfectly safe, use a rule of two. It takes twice as long to do anything as you think it will.

Buying a lot and building your own house is a wonderful experience. But as anyone who has done it will tell you, it's the sort of thing most people only want to do once!

15

What to Look For in a Home Inspection

You need to have good, detailed information on the condition of the home you are buying. After all, just because it's standing today doesn't mean that it isn't ready to fall over tomorrow.

In the past, the dictum "Let the buyer beware!" was the rule in house hunting. Today, however, consumerism has turned the tables. Today it's "Let the seller beware." Sellers in many areas of the country must present to you, the buyer, a disclosure listing any and all faults with the house, often at the time you first see it or at least at the time you make a purchase offer. (In California, for example, you have three days to evaluate the disclosure statement. If you're given the disclosure after the seller has accepted your offer, you may have grounds for backing out of the deal for up to three days.)

Further, sellers now expect a buyer to insist on a professional home inspection. After all, it protects the seller, in many cases, even more than you! The reason is that while sellers may know many of the home's problems (such as a leaky roof or broken window), they may know next to nothing about the house's heating system or its foundation.

TIP—ASK FOR PREVIOUS INSPECTION REPORTS

Sellers should keep and present to you any previous reports, including those they obtained when they purchased the home as well as any from previous buyers who didn't complete the purchase. They can reveal much.

183

For that reason, many sellers are glad to have an inspector's report to go along with their disclosure statement. It shows they have diligently made an effort to learn about problems and disclose them.

TRAP—YOU PAY FOR IT

Expect to pay for your home inspection, probably around $250 to $350. And usually the inspector wants to be paid at the time the inspection is completed, sometimes in cash! Make sure to arrange for how you'll pay in advance so you don't get a nasty surprise.

The time to insist on a home inspection is when you make your initial offer. Write it into the sales agreement. Make sure that it's a contingency of the purchase. (See Chapter 10 for a description of contingency clauses.)

Sellers are almost universally prepared to let you have a home inspection. But they won't let you tie up their property indefinitely. Typically they will limit your inspection contingency by insisting that it be completed and your approval given within 14 days. If you don't approve, the deal's off and the house is back on the market. Indeed, many sellers will insist that they be able to continue showing the house and to accept backup offers until you remove the inspection contingency.

Where Do I Find a Home Inspector?

Ask your real estate agent. Usually active agents know of several they can recommend. However, also follow through on the recommendations suggested below. You don't want to hire an inspector recommended by an agent because he or she has a track record of going easy on the property, thereby helping to make the deal go through.

Also ask the lender or the escrow officer. As a last resort, try the phone book.

When you select an inspector, ask if he or she is a member of ASHI (American Society of Home Inspectors) *www.ashi.com* or

NAHI (National Association of Home Inspectors) *www.nahi.org.* It doesn't guarantee competence, but it indicates they at least belong to national trade associations.

TRAP—YOU MAY GET AN
UNLICENSED INSPECTOR

At this point home inspectors are not yet licensed in most states. That means that anyone—you, I, or the guy who sold you this book—may be able to hang out a shingle and be an inspector. That means it's up to you to be sure you're dealing with someone competent.

Check Out Your Inspector

Ask your future inspector for at least three referrals from past jobs. Then call those people. Hopefully, it will be at least six months or more since the inspection and they will have had an opportunity to see if something came up that wasn't initially discovered.

You may get some surprising answers.

Check the inspector's credentials: What qualifies him or her to be an inspector? Look for someone with a related degree and a broad building background such as a soils or structural engineer. Often retired county or city building inspectors make great choices.

TRAP—BE WARY OF FORMER
CONTRACTORS

Some former contractors make money on the side as inspectors. That's okay, but just because a person has a contractor's license doesn't mean he or she knows anything about a home inspection. A plumbing contractor, for example, may be able to do a great job checking out your sinks and toilets. But the contractor may know next to nothing about the wiring.

Should I Go Along with the Inspection?

It's the only way you can really learn what the home's problems are. An inspection is both oral and written. In the oral part, the inspector describes problems to you as you go through, under, and over the home. You can ask questions and can often get useful information on how to correct a problem as well as how much that correction will cost.

A written report, on the other hand, is often more formal. These days many inspectors are afraid to write down any but the most glaring of problems for fear that they could be sued by the seller for exaggerating something. Hence, the written reports tend to be bland and, quite frankly, not that useful. Often they are filled with more disclaimers than information. That's why you need to go along and listen to what the inspector says. Here are just a few warning signs (there are many others) that you can watch out for:

Warning Signs of Bad Defects

- "V" shaped cracks in the foundation—indicates serious cracking
- Offsetting cracks in the foundation—indicates serious cracking
- Cracks in interior walls—suggests structural problems, bad foundation
- Water marks on the roof rafters—indicates a leaking roof
- Water marks on basement walls—indicates seasonal flooding
- Standing water under home—indicates poor drainage, possible foundation problems to come
- Slanted floors—suggests bad foundation or structural damage

The inspector will point things out. But your inspector might not be the best in the world, so you should have an idea what to look for yourself. Below is a home inspection checklist. Use it as a guide either with an inspector or, if you're bolder, when you inspect the property yourself. Keep in mind that while it offers many ideas, it is not complete. There may be problems with the property beyond the scope of the checklist.

TRAP—IT'S NOT SELF-HELP TIME

Don't try to do an inspection on your own unless you know a great deal about buildings. I've been inspecting properties for more than 30 years and I still always hire a professional inspector to go along with me. The engineer can point out things that I miss, and vice versa.

Home Inspection Checklist

Drainage

Drainage problems can lead to cracked foundations and slabs. They can cause a house to shift, particularly if it's located on a hillside, and in extreme cases can cause the actual collapse of the home. The correction of drainage problems is best left to experts. However, even a beginner can usually tell where drainage problems exist.

Drainage Checklist

	YES	NO
▪ Is there dampness under the house? (The basement should be dry as dust.)	[ ]	[ ]
▪ Are there footprints or ribbed patterns in the dirt under the house, indicating that when it rains, water creeps in?	[ ]	[ ]
▪ Is there mold (black or green) on wood under the house, indicating heavy moisture? (There's almost a hysteria these days about black mold—check with your agent.)	[ ]	[ ]
▪ Does the ground outside slope *away* from the house? (If it slopes into the house, you've got serious problems.)	[ ]	[ ]

Foundation

The concrete foundation is what supports your house. Usually there is a peripheral foundation that goes around the entire edge of the home. Within this peripheral foundation there may be concrete blocks holding up piers that support the floor (in a wood floor home) or a concrete slab (in a cement floor home). The peripheral foundation typically has "footings" that extend downward perhaps two feet or more. (In freezing climates the footings should be below the freeze line.)

The further down the foundation extends and the wider it is, the better. In areas with expansive soil (the soil swells when wet) or other soil problems, the concrete foundation should be deep and wide enough to survive any expansion of the soil. In addition, there should be steel rods ("rebars" or reinforcement bars) in the concrete. The steel holds the concrete together. (Cement by itself, even with the new plasticizers and fibers, will tend to crack.)

Cracks in the foundation can lead to uneven floors inside the house. It can also lead to slippage down a hillside as well as to broken windows and cracks appearing in walls and ceilings. Some breakage of foundations happens naturally over time. However, severe breakage indicates a problem that could get worse.

Foundation Checklist

	YES	NO
■ Do you see cracks in the foundation when you walk around the exterior of the house? (Hairline cracks always occur and usually can be disregarded.)	[ ]	[ ]
■ Are the cracks wider at the top than at the bottom? (This indicates actual breakage, a serious problem.)	[ ]	[ ]
■ Is there an actual separation in the foundation? (This indicates that not enough steel reinforcement was used when the foundation was built.)	[ ]	[ ]
■ In a slab house, does the floor feel uneven when you walk over it (indicating cracks hidden under carpets or tiles)?	[ ]	[ ]
■ Under a house, do any of the girders sag (a sign that the foundation has slipped)?	[ ]	[ ]

Roof

The purpose of the roof, besides providing an aesthetic look, is to keep rain and snow out of the house. The cost of repairing a roof can be high, of replacing a roof enormous ($5000 to $25,000 or more depending on the materials used). You want to be sure that the roof is in good shape. If it's not, you may want to have the seller fix or replace it or make an adjustment to the price.

Some general information on roofs is in order.

Wood Shake Roofs.   Depending on the thickness of the shake, they can last 20 to 30 years. If the house you are buying has a wood shake roof and it's 20 years old or older, check the roof very carefully.

Wood Shake Roof Checklist

	YES	NO
■ Are there pieces of the roof lying on the ground around the house? (This is an obvious bad sign.)	[ ]	[ ]
■ Using binoculars, can you see missing shingles anywhere on the roof?	[ ]	[ ]
■ Are the shingles intact? (Badly cracked shingles are another bad sign.)	[ ]	[ ]
■ Are there any signs of leakage in the ceiling or walls inside the house? Go into the attic and look up. If it's daytime and you see light pouring through many tiny or large holes, you've got trouble.	[ ]	[ ]

Composition Shingles.   Made of tar, fiberglass, or some similar composition, they have a life span of 15 to 30 years, depending on the quality and materials.

Composition Roof Checklist

	YES	NO
■ Is the *color* of the shingles good? (Fading shingles are a sign of wear.)	[ ]	[ ]
■ Are the edges of the shingles curling up? (This is a sign of wear in hot climates.)	[ ]	[ ]
■ Are there any bare spots on the roof?	[ ]	[ ]
■ Are there any signs of leakage in the ceiling or walls inside the house.	[ ]	[ ]

Aluminum Shingles.   These have a life span of 50 years or so. Generally they don't wear out unless they have been damaged.

Aluminum Shingle Checklist

	YES	NO
▪ Are there signs of peeling or fading of their color? (The shingles may continue to keep the weather out, but will look terrible.)	[ ]	[ ]
▪ Are there any dents or separations in the shingles, indicating someone has walked on them?	[ ]	[ ]
▪ Are there any signs of leakage in the ceiling or walls inside the house?	[ ]	[ ]

Tile Shingles.   Tile roofs last indefinitely (80 years or more). However, they can easily be broken, and once broken they quickly lose their ability to keep the weather out. *Don't walk on tile roofs—you'll break the tiles.*

Tile Roof Checklist

	YES	NO
▪ Are any of the tiles broken?	[ ]	[ ]
▪ Have any fallen off?	[ ]	[ ]
▪ Are there any signs of leakage in the ceiling or walls inside the house?	[ ]	[ ]

Paint

Interior.   In a resale, don't expect to get a house that doesn't require repainting. As noted in an earlier chapter, as soon as the seller's furniture gets moved out, you're going to see whole areas that need repainting. The only question is: Will you do it or will the seller?

Interior Paint Checklist

	YES	NO
▪ Are there marks on the walls?	[ ]	[ ]
▪ Is the current paint flaking, indicating it will have to be sanded before new paint can be applied?	[ ]	[ ]

- Are the colors light or dark? (Covering dark colors may
  require two or more new coats.)   [ ]   [ ]
- Is there lead in the paint? (You may want to have it tested.
  Homes painted prior to 1978 often have lead paint in them.
  Your agent should be able to suggest a lead testing company
  nearby or check with www.epa.gov.)   [ ]   [ ]

Exterior.   Weathering is the problem here. Even the best paints
usually don't last more than five to seven years. Repainting the
exterior can be more expensive than painting the interior, since it
often requires removing chipped and peeling paint.

Exterior Paint Checklist

	YES	NO
- Is the paint chipped or peeling?	[ ]	[ ]
- Are the colors faded? (Faded colors indicate paint that is aging.)	[ ]	[ ]
- Is the caulking around windows starting to fall out?	[ ]	[ ]
- Is the paint on the gutters or siding peeling?	[ ]	[ ]

Plumbing

In general, you need an expert to tell you if there are serious
plumbing problems. There are, however, some telltale signs you can
check for.

Plumbing Checklist

	YES	NO
- Is the plumbing galvanized steel? (Galvanized steel lasts about 30 years, sometimes less. Copper lasts virtually forever.)	[ ]	[ ]
- Are there leaks at the joints of galvanized pipes? (Usually visible under the house or in the garage, leaks indicate that electrolytic action may be corroding the pipes and they could need to be replaced—$5000 or more for the whole house.)	[ ]	[ ]
- Are there leaks under the sinks in any of the bathrooms or kitchen? (Possibly a minor problem, but why should you have to fix it?)	[ ]	[ ]

- Is the water heater old? (The date is sometimes stamped on the label—a water heater rarely lasts more than 7 to 10 years in areas with silt in the water or high electrolytic action.)   [ ]   [ ]
- Does the water heater have a temperature/pressure safety valve? (This is vitally important. If you're not sure what a safety valve is, have a professional check it out.)   [ ]   [ ]

In addition, the gas supply line needs to be checked. A professional should do this.

Wiring

This is the venue of the professional. Don't attempt to make a judgment on the wiring unless you're an electrician. Some danger signals to watch for include switches or sockets that spark when used and inoperative lights or switches. *Never attempt to check any electrical item unless the power is completely off!*

Heating

Even more so than in the case of wiring, a professional needs to check out the heating. If you're using gas, you need to be sure that there are no leaks. Some telltale signs to look for include smelling burned gas fumes coming from heating vents and yellow flames in the furnace that rise above the burners (These are bad signs indicating a leak in the heat exchanger, a dangerous condition usually requiring replacement of the furnace—$2500 or more.) Also, if you smell gas around the furnace it's a very dangerous sign—call the gas company immediately.)

Fireplace

Most people figure that there's little to go wrong with a fireplace. Unfortunately, that's not the case. The bricks in a fireplace can crack and the fireplace itself can pull away from the house (something that happens in earthquake country). Even more serious, the interior casing can break, allowing dangerous gases to enter the house. A bad fireplace is a dangerous situation that can lead to house fires, poisoning, or asphyxiation. Have a professional check it out.

Fireplace Checklist

	YES	NO
■ From the outside, is there a separation between the fireplace and the house? (A separation is a big danger sign.)	[ ]	[ ]
■ Are there any visible cracks in the external bricks of the fireplace?	[ ]	[ ]
■ Are there any cracks in the firebricks inside the fireplace?	[ ]	[ ]
■ Does the flue work?	[ ]	[ ]

Tile

Tile problems are usually easily spotted because they consist mostly of cracks in the tiles or staining of the grout.

Tile Checklist

	YES	NO
■ Are there any cracks in the tile of the kitchen or bathrooms? (Cracks can simply be caused by dropping something heavy on the tile, or they can be symptomatic of broken cabinets, house movements, or even a cracked foundation.)	[ ]	[ ]
■ Are floor tiles cracked? (Replacing cracked floor tiles when there is a problem with the floor simply means that the new tiles will soon crack. Fixing the underlying floor problem could be very expensive.)	[ ]	[ ]

What Do I Do with the Termite Report?

When you get a new loan, the lender almost always requires a termite clearance. This is a report from a registered termite company that states that the house is free of infestation.

It's important to understand that the report is of limited value. In areas where termites are endemic, there will almost always be some infestation. (The report usually states the house to be clear of termites for 60 to 180 days—the inspectors know that after that the termites likely will be back.)

In order to get a clearance, repair work must often be done. In some cases this is minor, involving the replacement of some wood and occasionally spraying. In other cases it is major, requiring the tenting of the house. Modern techniques may involve freezing the termites out of localized areas. In most cases the termites chomp away at the wood structure of the home and are of little consequence. The real problem is that over 30 or 40 years, they can eat enough of the wood to make the house collapse.

Usually the seller will pay for any corrective work. You, however, will likely be responsible for any preventative work, but that is at your option. (You usually aren't required to do it.)

What About Environmental Hazards?

Thus far we've been dealing with typical problems that you can look for in any home. There are, however, additional problems that may be of a hazardous nature. You should be aware of these and have a professional check for them.

Also, certain parts of the country are now requiring buyer and seller to sign off on some of these problems as well as other potential hazards. Be sure to check with your real estate agent about any conditions on the sale that the city, county, or state may impose. Additionally, there may be federal requirements, as is the case with lead.

Asbestos?

Prior to about 1980, blown-in ceilings sometimes contained asbestos fibers. If you're worried abut them, these ceilings may have to be scraped and removed or encapsulated with a sealant and a nonasbestos mixture. The cost for this can be high.

In some parts of the country, heating pipes under the house or in the basement were wrapped in asbestos insulation. If disturbed, this may need to be removed by experts and the pipes rewrapped.

Asbestos can also occur in other areas such as tile floors. A good inspection will thoroughly check for it.

Smoke Alarms?

These should be installed on all floors and near kitchens and fireplaces as well as in every bedroom.

Insulation?

This isn't really a hazard. However, if you're in cold country without adequate insulation, you can be mighty uncomfortable. Adding new insulation to an older home can be a problem. While roof insulation usually can easily be blown in, for walls, it's much more difficult. In some areas, holes were cut and a formaldehyde-based insulation shot into the walls. However, formaldehyde itself is a health hazard, and where this has been done, sometimes the walls must be cut open and the insulation removed. Check with a good insulation company in your area regarding your options.

Earthquake Retrofitting?

In some parts of the country, particularly the West Coast, new laws are being proposed and are coming on line that may eventually require sellers to retrofit older homes and bring them up to earthquake safety standards.

This may be something as simple as tying the framing down to the foundation or as complex as putting steel reinforcements from the foundation up to the roof. Be sure to check out what's necessary in your area and have the seller do the expensive work.

Flood Plain?

Some homes are built on a flood plain. It may not flood more than once every 50 or 100 years. But if you're the owner during that year, you lose. Often insurance is hard to get and expensive. Check it out.

Radon Gas Hazard?

Radon is a naturally occurring gas in many soils In some areas it can leak out of the ground and accumulate in the basement, and sometimes in other areas, of a house. It is a health hazard.

This is something that should be checked, particularly if you are in an area where radon gas leakage is common. Simple testing kits are available for under $50.

If radon gas is a problem, an environmental engineer should be contacted to determine how it can be eliminated from the home. Often, increasing the ventilation in a basement will do the trick.

Other times expensive electronic venting systems are needed. In a very few cases, it may be impossible to eliminate the hazard, in which case you may want to look elsewhere.

Lead Paint Hazard?

If the house you are considering was built before the late 1970s (when lead paint was banned), chances are lead paint was used both inside and out. Lead is a serious health threat. It can produce sickness, retardation, and in extreme cases, even death. The most common means of getting lead poisoning is when children chew on molding or other painted areas of a house and ingest the lead paint.

Sometimes old exterior paint containing lead will flake or dust off and contaminate the ground around the outside of the house where children play, and they may ingest some of the soil. By federal mandate, the seller must present you with a disclosure statement regarding this hazard. (However, this statement often simply says that the seller is unaware of the lead hazard in the property, throwing it back in your court.)

Safely removing lead paint is difficult and requires a qualified specialist. It can easily cost $10,000 or more to remove it properly from a home. On the other hand, people sometimes simply paint over the lead paint with a nontoxic modern paint and hope for the best. Unfortunately, encapsulation is not an approved method of dealing with lead paint. Few sellers are willing to pop for the cost of removing lead paint.

Thus the choice becomes yours—are you willing to live in a house with this hazard? Many buyers of older homes who are made aware of the lead paint problem through the disclosure statement do move forward with the deal, especially if they don't have young children. If this problem worries you, opt for a newer home.

Leaded Copper Pipe Joints?

Prior to about 1986, the solder used to connect copper pipes in houses was made of a mixture of tin and lead. It was discovered that the lead would sometimes leach into water that sat in the pipes. (Modern solders use a nonlead mixture.) There is little that can be done about this, short of resoldering all the copper joints. However, after about five years the leaching process tends to become minimal. It's mostly a problem in leading joint piping houses that are less than five years old. (You can run the water a while before using it to reduce the risk of lead poisoning.)

Black Mold

This is the hazard de jour in many areas. Black mold has been around since time immemorial. However, some have suggested that a new more toxic variety is now attacking houses. Thus CDC (Center for Disease Control) and many state environmental agencies are conducting studies to see if black mold poses a serious health hazard, but the results were not available as of this writing. Certainly some people are allergic to molds in general.

The problem is that a kind of hysteria has surrounded homes that contain black mold. This is a serious problem because most homes in wet climates tend to have it. Therefore, you should have the house checked for black mold. While you yourself may not find it objectionable, it could mean trouble when you try to resell to the next buyer. Finding serious black mold should weigh into your purchase decision.

Other Environmental Hazards

These can be anything from formaldehyde odors to copper in the drinking water. Ask your inspector about these and any other environmental hazards that may be present.

Having your home professionally inspected is an important part of the purchase process. Don't skimp on it.

16

How to Avoid Getting Gouged at Closing

Nobody wants to pay closing costs. They are the transaction costs of buying real estate that we all would rather do without. Nevertheless, closing costs do exist, and sometimes they are abused.

It's important to understand that closing costs are not completely regulated. Lenders can sometimes charge what they want, leading to so-called "garbage fees" or unnecessary charges that only benefit the lender. (What are garbage fees is open to interpretation—I give you my take on it throughout this chapter.) On the other hand, there are rules that lenders need to live by.

Under RESPA (Real Estate Settlement Procedures Act), a lender must give you a good-faith estimate of what your costs for the loan, and in effect the transaction, will be within three days of your making a formal application. Giving you notice, however, does not necessarily mean reducing those costs or even being totally accurate.

In addition HUD (Department of Housing and Urban Development) requires that a HUD-1 statement of your closing expenses be given to you, but not until within one day of closing. By then, of course, it's usually too late to do anything about the costs.

New Changes to Closing Procedures

Because current closing procedures have produced so many problems and complaints, HUD has indicated it may adopt a two-tiered system (not yet in effect as of this writing). Under this plan there would be two kinds of closing costs:

- GFE—Good Faith Estimate. This is pretty much the old system where the lender can give you an estimate that may or may not prove to be accurate.
- GMPA—Guaranteed Mortgage Package Agreement. Here the lender guarantees that the closing costs will be no more than a set amount. However, that amount could be higher than the estimate given under the other plan.

In addition, there is some thought being given to identifying the various lender fees (which compose most of the closing costs for the buyer) and codifying these. Nevertheless, it behooves every buyer to examine what the closing costs might be to see where they can be reduced.

Here's a list of typical closing costs when purchasing a home. (*Note:* You probably won't have all of these; you may have most of them.)

Typical Closing Costs Checklist

- Hazard insurance policy (fire insurance)
- Homeowner's insurance home warranty package
- Tax prorations
- Tax service contract
- Mortgage fees
- Attorney fee
- Escrow fee
- Title insurance fee
- A variety of other fees may also be imposed

Most buyers are confused by these fees, so let's go over some of the more common ones.

TIP—THE BEST LEGAL DEAL IN TOWN

The attorneys who work in real estate usually have set fees for standard transactions. These fees are normally between $500 and $1500, depending on the size and complexity of the deal. Be sure you discuss the fees before hiring an attorney. Remember, the attorney fees, like everything else, are negotiable.

Why Do I Have to Pay for Hazard Insurance?

As the buyer of a home (new or resale) you will want to carry fire insurance. This insures you, and the lender, that in the event of a catastrophe, the home can be rebuilt.

Don't think you can save money by just taking a chance and not insuring the property. The lender will demand that you carry minimum fire insurance as a condition of the financing. If you don't, the lender will put its own, usually more expensive policy on the property and bill you for it. If you refuse to pay, you could be placed in default and the lender could foreclose.

While you are required to pay for fire and basic hazard insurance, you are not usually required to carry a "homeowner's policy" (although some lenders do now require it). The homeowner's policy runs almost twice as much as the basic fire/hazard policy, but it's a good investment. It protects you against a variety of losses, including liability if someone gets hurt on your property.

TRAP—CAN YOU GET HAZARD INSURANCE?

In some areas of the country, insurers have recently been refusing to issue new policies because of losses. Be sure to check to see that you can actually get insurance, or else you might not be able to conclude the purchase of your home!

What's a Home Warranty Package?

A home warranty package is optional. It typically costs from $250 upward annually, depending on the quality of coverage.

The plan covers problems with many of your home's systems, such as electrical and plumbing. Most sellers will pay for the first year, to keep you from calling to complain about something such as a leaking water heater. You can usually continue the plan in subsequently years by paying the premium yourself.

Why Do I Have to Pay Taxes on My Purchase?

It's the only thing that's certain, besides death! You do not have to pay sales tax (at least not yet!) in any area of the country that I know of, although some states do charge a usually nominal "transfer tax." But you do have to pay property taxes. The escrow company prorates your share of the year's taxes. Proration simply means that if the sellers have already paid taxes in advance, you pay them back for that portion of time that you own the property.

If you are getting a new loan that has a tax impound account, the lender may also require that you pay one or two month's worth of taxes up front to get the account started. (This account pays your taxes for you each year.)

TIP—YOU COULD GET DINGED FOR A "TAX SERVICE CONTRACT"

If you don't have an impound account, the lender will undoubtedly want you to pay for a service that will report any time you fail to pay your taxes. This is so the lender can then step in, pay them, and then foreclose on you! The fee is usually around $25 to $50. And there's no getting out of it!

Why Do I Have to Pay Mortgage Fees?

If you get a new mortgage, you're going to have to pay closing fees on it. These usually compose the largest part of the closing costs. Often the costs of closing the mortgage can come to as much as 4 or 5 percent or more of the total purchase price. Here are some of the fees and what they represent:

Mortgage Closing Costs Fees Checklist

- Assumption Fee—If you're assuming an existing mortgage, you will undoubtedly have to pay a fee. It's typically in the $100 or less range. However, most loans today are not assumable.

- Document Preparation Fee—A garbage fee paid to the lender for preparing the loan documents. Since the lender is making the loan and since it takes only a few taps on a computer keyboard to spit out the documents, in this author's opinion it's absurd to charge a high fee for it.

- Points—A point is equal to 1 percent of the mortgage. If the mortgage is for $100,000, 2 points is equal to $2000. Lenders charge points for a variety of reasons, usually to offset a lower-than-market interest rate that you may be getting. The amount of points you pay varies according to the market. I've seen points as high as 10 and as low as zero. Be sure you shop around before you secure financing from the lender offering the lowest points. (See Chapter 5.) The points you pay to get a home loan may be considered interest and may be deductible from your annual income tax. The rule for this, however, seems to change frequently, so check with your tax accountant to see how much, if any, may be deductible.

- Loan Fee—The loan fee is an up-front charge in addition to points. Many lenders, for example, will charge "2 points plus $600." The $600 is the loan fee and usually goes to cover such work as preparing documents and funding the money. Of course, it's preposterous to pay points as well as a loan fee and a document preparation fee. A good lender will not charge these, or will charge only a minimal loan fee. All the costs should be up front, where you can clearly see them.

- Account Setup Fee—Some lenders may charge you to set up the payback account, the little payment book or monthly invoices you'll get when you pay. This is another garbage fee.

- Impound Account and Setup/Service Fee—Some loans require you to pay one-twelfth of your taxes and insurance each month. "Impound" simply means the holding of tax and insurance money for you (and then paying it out appropriately). Recent legislation has required lenders to be more scrupulous as to how they handle impound accounts and to demand only a minimum amount of money, usually no more than a month or two, for the account. Some lenders, however, will charge you for setting up this account. Again, to my way of thinking, this is a ridiculous charge.

- Attorney Fee—If it's your attorney, then of course you will need to pay the fee. On the other hand, if it's the lender's attorney for checking over the mortgage documents and the transaction, it's probably another garbage fee. Unless the deal is unusual in some way, the lender should have attorneys on staff—virtually all do—who automatically check documents and deals. It should be part of the lending service, not a separate charge.

- Collection Setup Fee—A collection setup fee is usually charged if part of the property is a rental and rents need to be collected and paid directly to the lender, or if your payment is going to be paid directly out of your paycheck or checking account to the lender. This fee is atypical and shouldn't appear unless the lender discusses special circumstances with you in advance.

- Recording Fees—The escrow company charges fees for recording documents. They are usually under $25 apiece. It's a garbage fee if the lender wants to charge you a second time for the same fee.

- Lender's Escrow—The lender may insist on a separate escrow for the mortgage. If so, this is the fee. Ask in advance and go with a different lender if it is exorbitant.

- Lender's Title Insurance—The lender may require a more comprehensive policy of title insurance called an ALTA. If so, this is the charge.

- Additional charges that lenders throw in. They can be very creative.

What Is Title Insurance?

This insures the property against a deficient title from the time you buy it going backward. It means that if a past seller forged a signature or there was a lien that wasn't paid, the insurance should cover it.

TRAP—WHOSE TITLE COMPANY IS IT, ANYWAY?

There are lots of title insurance companies. Sometimes the agent will prefer a specific company. That may be because the title company is giving them perks or because the real estate agency owns the title company. (Perks might be something as innocuous as free stationery.) The relationship between the title company and the agent should be disclosed to you and you should be given the option of going elsewhere. Since for practical purposes one title company is usually as good as another, it really shouldn't matter to you—except in the case of fees. If one title company is cheaper than another, I would insist on the cheaper company. You must do this at the time escrow is opened.

How Is the Division of Closing Costs between Buyer and Seller Handled?

Usually the party (buyer or seller) who pays for the escrow and title insurance is determined by custom in the particular area. Sometimes it is customary to split these costs with the seller. Other times, either the seller or the buyer pays all of them. You will be pressured to follow custom for your area. You don't have to, however. Remember, virtually everything is negotiable in real estate.

As part of the escrow charges there may also be other prorations of interest, taxes, rents, and insurance. Just be sure that you're paying only your fair share. Check with your agent, attorney, or accountant if you're not sure.

Items typically are prorated at the close of escrow. However, if you are not getting possession of the property until a later date, then it's unfair for you to have to pay interest, insurance, and taxes until that date. If you're taking possession later than the close of escrow, be sure that prorations are made as of that later date.

How Do I Avoid Garbage Fees?

There are two ways, both of which have already been suggested. First, know what the costs and fees should be. If you can't recognize a garbage fee, how can you challenge it?

Second, demand that all garbage fees be eliminated or at the least reduced. However, you must do this at the opening of escrow. If you wait until the deal is ready to close to try to make changes, you could endanger your loan, which could mean no deal and a very angry seller.

If the lender won't dismiss garbage charges when you bring them up at the time of applying for a loan, get a different lender. There are no shortages of lenders in the country.

How Do I Get the Seller to Pay My Closing Costs?

Remember, everything in real estate is negotiable! That includes closing costs.

To have the seller pay yours, make it a contingency of the purchase. If the seller doesn't pay, you don't buy. The trick, of course, is getting the seller to go along. In a strong market, sellers will simply show your agent (who's presenting the deal) to the door. They won't consider it.

In a weak market, however, where the sellers have been trying unsuccessfully to get out of their house for six months, it may work. The key is to find a seller who's highly motivated to sell. If you're the only buyer to come by in a long while, you may get them to pay your closing costs.

Other considerations are when you're giving that seller a better price than he or she anticipated, or better terms. In a trade-off, the seller might consider paying your closing costs.

TIP—TRADE CLOSING COSTS
FOR CASH

Remember, the closing costs are cash. However, sometimes they can be financed. You offer the seller a good price (assuming the property appraises out) and get a big loan, sometimes for the full value of the home (see Chapter 4). In return, the seller pays your cash closing costs.

Of course, some buyers who are very tough negotiators argue for it all—good price, good terms, and seller pays closing costs! As I said, in a bad market where houses just aren't selling, sometimes desperate sellers will agree.

How Do I Wrap the Closing Costs into the Mortgage?

Finally, it may be possible to wrap the closing costs into the mortgage. Many lenders these days offer "no cost" mortgages. You could opt for one.

A "no cost" mortgage is a misnomer. There are costs. It's just that they are hidden. For example, I recently obtained such a mortgage. At closing, the lender paid all of my NRCC (nonrecurring closing costs), which included title, escrow, and lender's fees. (It did not, of course, pay my recurring costs such as prorations and hazard insurance.)

In exchange for doing this, the lender increased the interest rate, by 3/8 of a percent.

I had a choice. I could pay the closing costs in cash. Or I could pay a slightly higher interest rate (and slightly higher monthly payment) and have no NRCC.

Other lenders will roll the closing costs into the mortgage. In other words, they will give you the same interest rate, but you'll end up owing more. The closing costs will be added to the mortgage.

Either way, it's an effective method of reducing the amount of cash you have to come up with at closing. Just remember that the downside is either a higher interest rate or a bigger loan, both of which usually translate into slightly higher monthly payments.

Closing costs are the bane of real estate transactions. To avoid a bad surprise late in the deal, be sure to get good estimates of what they are.

For more information on closing costs and "garbage fees" check into, *The Homebuyer's Closing Checklist,* McGraw-Hill, 2003.

17

Everyone's Flipping Over Real Estate

A recent buzzword in real estate is "flipping." It essentially means selling a property as soon as you buy it. In some cases, even before you buy it!

I'm sure that if you've heard the term, you've wondered if you, too, could do this. The answer is, yes, you can. But, and it's a BIG BUT, you have to find a property that will work as a "flipper."

What works as a flipper? Simple—any property that you can buy below market value. If you can find a property that's selling for less than it's worth (hopefully far less), you may be able to quickly flip it—resell it to someone else. And pocket the difference, usually in cash. Thus you would have a choice—buy it and move in yourself. Or do a rapid resale.

TRAP—THERE MAY BE TAXES TO PAY

 Don't think that because of the all the hype surrounding the big tax exclusion on homes, you won't have taxes on a flip. You almost certainly will. Remember, you must have lived in the home as your personal residence two out five years to get the up to $250,000 per person exclusion. You probably won't even get a capital gains tax rate because you won't have owned the property for at least a year. Check with your accountant.

How Do I Find a Property I Can Flip?

That's the big question everyone wants answered. If you're looking to buy a home to live in, my suggestion is forget about it. You've got enough to worry about in finding a good property.

On the other hand, if a flipper falls into your lap, don't let it go. Take full advantage of it.

How Do I Actually Flip a Property?

The mechanics of the deal can be complicated, particularly for novices. Basically, it goes something like this.

Once you locate a suitable property, you present a below-market offer. If the seller accepts, you now must quickly resell. Depending on how your offer was structured, your time period can be anywhere from a minimum of about 30 days to a maximum of about six months.

You then bring in a rebuyer (one who actually purchases the property) who concludes the sale with the original seller. The rebuyer puts up the cash down payment and closing costs and gets new financing. A portion of the purchase price goes to cash out the original seller. And you get the remainder, usually in cash, but sometimes in the form of a second mortgage, for yourself.

There are basically two methods of structuring your purchase: the assignment and the option.

How Do I Offer an Option?

Real estate options are not much different from stock options. For the buyer, they are an opportunity (but not a requirement) to purchase for a set price at some future date. For the seller, they are a commitment to sell for a set price at a set date.

Note, an option is not a purchase. Rather you are buying an option on the property—getting the right, but not the obligation, to purchase sometime in the future. For this privilege you would normally give the seller some option money, perhaps $1000 to $5000 or more. (The further out the option date, the more money is usually required.)

TIP—IT'S AT YOUR OPTION

Note that in an option, you the buyer are *not* committed to purchase. It's at your discretion. The seller, however, is committed to sell. He or she must go through with the transaction, IF you execute your option.

Why would a seller agree to such a thing? Cash! Remember, you usually put up some option money, which the seller gets to keep if you don't eventually make the purchase.

The term of the option is likewise negotiable. Usually they run from 30 days to six months or longer. When flipping a house, a term of 30 to 90 days would not be uncommon.

Pros and Cons of the Option

- You've tied up the property at a fixed price.
- You don't have to qualify for or obtain a mortgage. You also don't have to come up with a down payment.
- You don't own the property, so you're not responsible for mortgage payments, taxes, insurance, maintenance, or repairs.
- You've got a relatively small amount of cash tied up.
- But the money you put up is at risk if you can't find a rebuyer and exercise your option. If you don't exercise your option before it expires, you lose your option money (the amount you put up).
- If property values go down during the option period, you'll have trouble finding a buyer.

How Do I Assign My Purchase?

Assignment is the other method of flipping, often preferred by professionals. Here you make an offer to purchase, usually for cash. However, when you make your offer, you state that the buyer is your name "or assigns" or whatever language is appropriate in you state. What this means is that either you can buy the property, or anyone else you assign the contract to can buy the property.

Unlike the option, the assignment only runs for as long as a normal closing, typically 30 to 45 days. That means that you've got to find a buyer and conclude your other end of the deal very quickly.

Hopefully you have done your homework and have a rebuyer waiting in the wings. You now sign a separate agreement for the property with the rebuyer, but of course your sale is for a higher price. When the deal is ready to close, the rebuyer's name goes on the deed.

Again, you never actually make the purchase. The transaction is basically handled in escrow. At the end of the deal, you get your money out, typically in cash

The biggest problem with using an assignment is often getting a seller to accept. Savvy sellers won't always agree. The reason is that they don't know who will eventually purchase the property. They are afraid that you might not be able to get a needed mortgage and want a back door out, or that you're planning to sell your contract to someone else (which is, in fact, the case!) and that person may not qualify for a needed mortgage. In order to calm the seller's fears, you may need to put up a bigger deposit, or avoid putting many escape clauses (contingencies) into the contract, which can increase your risks.

Pros and Cons of the Assignment

- You only have to put up the original deposit when you buy the property from the seller, and you get this back from your rebuyer.
- If it works, it's a quick deal.
- No mortgage, property taxes, or insurance to worry about.
- But you actually do commit to purchasing the property. To protect yourself from having to complete the purchase in case you can't find a buyer (or your rebuyer falls through), you'll want lots of escape clauses (contingencies—see Chapter 10). But escape clauses weaken your offer and lessen your chances of getting it accepted. So to make the deal, you may have to take a big risk.
- If not handled properly, you can make the seller seriously mad at you and you can land yourself in a lawsuit.
- The seller may not be able to complete the sale for any number of reasons, so you'll again need lots of escape clauses to protect yourself from the rebuyer. Again, such clauses weaken your resale agreement.

The Big Problem with Flipping

Almost all sellers have a kind of personal relationship with the buyer. They want to know who's buying their property. (This is even the case with lenders, which almost always insist on knowing exactly whom they're dealing with.) When you assign the purchase agreement, you break that bond. Many sellers, nevertheless, are willing to go along provided the deal concludes in a reasonable fashion. After all, they're still getting a sale out of it. Many lenders will not, so your rebuyer may have trouble getting needed financing.

Another problem occurs when the sellers discover that you're reselling the property at a substantial profit. This can make a seller most unhappy. After all, they conclude, what are you bringing to the deal? They feel that your profit should rightly go into their pocket.

As a result, you could have an angry seller on your hands who at the least refuses to sign off on the deal unless he or she gets more money, or at worst, wants to take you to court. Thus, to oil the waters, many investors who flip in this manner foolishly don't tell the seller. They think that what the sellers won't know won't hurt them.

Something similar happens in the case of the rebuyer. Will he or she get mad if they discover that they're paying much more for the property than you are?

Therein lies the rub. There shouldn't be anything illegal or even unethical in flipping property, *as long as all parties involved are made aware of what's happening.* However, when one party doesn't know what's going on, there's all kinds of opportunity for things to go wrong.

Making the Hard Choice

Therefore, to avoid ethical and possibly legal problems down the road, it's a good idea to let both rebuyer and seller know exactly what's happening early on in the deal. In other words, no matter how painful, lay all your cards out on the table—let them know how much you're making. And get their agreement in writing in case either party should later on have a failure of memory.

Of course, this is hard. Once either party knows, they may not be willing to move forward. However, it's better they find out before-hand, rather than afterward.

TRAP—BE WARY OF THE DOUBLE ESCROW

 A double escrow can be construed as having the purpose of deceiving the seller or rebuyer or both. The reason is that each party only sees his or her one escrow and, as a consequence, doesn't see the entire deal. This is another reason to be sure that all parties to the deal understand exactly what's happening.

Won't Being Above Board Squelch the Deal?

Maybe yes, maybe no. If the deal is right, it should all go well. If someone is being tricked, then letting them know will definitely squelch the deal. But then again, why would you want to trick anyone? It will only land you in hot water later on.

The right way to handle a flip is to be sure that all parties know what you're doing. Sometimes when they learn of it, they'll admire you for it. After all, remember that you're providing a sale for a seller who wants to get out. And you're providing a home for a buyer who wants to get in. Why shouldn't you be entitled to a profit for that? It's a win, win, win situation!

Beware of Manipulation

What's given flipping a bad name more than anything else over the past few years are unscrupulous buyers who have manipulated mort-gages, appraisals, and rebuyers. Rather than do the real work of the transaction, namely finding properties that are selling below market, they have purchased properties at actual market and then, through manipulation, sold them for above market to unwary buyers. This sometimes has been done in apparent collusion with lenders who secured higher appraisals than were warranted and made bigger loans than were justified. Sometimes these properties were sold to poor minority rebuyers who really didn't understand about market value or how high their payments would be. Subsequently, when these rebuyers couldn't make stiff payments, the houses were lost to foreclosure.

That's where the real trouble started. Almost all home mortgages are one way or another insured or guaranteed through the government or a government-related agency (FHA, VA, Fannie Mae, Freddie Mac, and so forth). When the government began taking these properties back, it found out what was happening and launched criminal investigations into the flippers. This is not something you ever want to have happen to you.

What About a Lease-Option?

This really has little to do with flipping. However, since we've already discussed the option here, it's appropriate to talk about a slightly different variety—the lease-option.

The purpose for the buyer is usually to get into a property that he or she can't afford to outright purchase. Therefore, the buyer proposes to rent it. However, in addition to renting it (the lease), the buyer also gets the seller to commit to selling it at some time in the future (the option), perhaps one to three years down the road.

If the seller accepts, the buyer moves in as a tenant. And later when the tenant has more cash, or a higher income, the tenant makes the purchase. Typically a portion of each month's rent goes toward the down payment. Of course, you'll want this portion to be as high as possible. Just remember, however, that until you are able to exercise the option, you are still just a tenant.

TRAP—BEWARE OF A HIGHER RENTAL

Sellers will often want to charge a higher-than-market rental for a lease-option. If they do, they should credit you with the difference between the market rental rate and that higher rent when it comes to exercising your option. Or give you back a portion if you decide not to exercise your option.

Who Can Handle the
Paperwork for Me?

There are a host of books out there on flipping. However, be wary of attempting to flip just based on what you read in them. Whether you get an option, a lease-option, or an assignment, you will need expert help. Be sure that you have a good attorney and a very experienced agent working with you.

This area is fraught with pitfalls. Yes, there are profits to be made. But you can also get yourself in serious trouble. If you're new to it, don't go it alone.

18

12 Steps to Quicker and Easier Home Buying

Imagine trying to win a game of football without knowing the rules. You'd send your team out into the field not knowing the difference between quarters or innings, how many points you would get for a touchdown or a field goal, or even which direction to run! It wouldn't matter how professional your team was. If you didn't know how the game was played, even a grammar school team could beat you.

Real estate is similar. Buying a home is not like buying anything else. It's not like buying a car, or a computer, or a jar of mayonnaise. It has its procedures, which in most cases are rigorously followed.

If you've bought a home before, you probably have a good idea of how it's done. But if it's been some time since you bought, or if this is going to be your first purchase, the process may seem mysterious, even arcane.

But not anymore. In quickstep, here are the 12 procedural motions you'll want to go through in making your purchase:

The 12 Steps to Making a Purchase

1. PRE-APPROVAL—You decide you want to buy (or at least want to look) and get pre-approved.
2. AGENT—Along the way you talk with one or more agents who show you properties.
3. OFFER—You find the home of your dreams (you hope!) and make a *written* offer on a document called a purchase agree-

ment, usually for less than the sellers are asking. (Verbal offers aren't illegal, just unenforceable.)

4. COUNTEROFFER—If the sellers don't accept, they may make a counteroffer, which you may in turn accept or decline, in which case you may then counter.

5. ACCEPTANCE—The sellers eventually accept your offer, or one of your counters. (If the sellers don't accept, start over with Step 1.)

6. ESCROW—Your agent or you open *escrow*. Used today in most states, it is a licensed and bonded company that acts as a neutral third party. The escrow holder receives all funds, makes sure that all documents are properly executed, and when all the conditions of the sales agreement (and the lender) have been met, transfers title to you, records the mortgage in favor of the lender, and gives the sellers their funds. Escrow typically lasts 30 to 60 days.

7. FINANCING—You secure your financing (if you haven't already) from the lender who pre-approved you, or some other lender.

8. APPROVALS—You approve (or disapprove) a home inspection. You approve (or disapprove) the seller's disclosures about defects in the home. If you disapprove, you may negotiate a lower price, get sellers to fix the problem, or get out of the deal, depending on how your purchase agreement was worded.

9. CONTINGENCIES—You fulfill any other obligations you're committed to as part of the sales agreement, such as putting extra cash into the deposit or approving a contingency. The sellers do likewise, such as providing a termite clearance, obtaining clear title, and clearing any contingencies they may have.

10. FUNDING—Your lender agrees to fund your mortgage.

11. WALK-THROUGH—You have a final "walk-through" inspection of the property. Then you sign the final documents (mostly loan papers); the escrow records the documents and transfers the funds.

12. POSSESSION—You get possession and the key.

19

12 Tips for Making Successful Counteroffers

Some people say that writing is, in reality, the art of rewriting. In real estate it's similar. Getting the deal you want isn't just in the offer you make, it's also in the counteroffer.

Counteroffers occur when the seller turns down your original offer, but then sends you back a sales agreement that offers different price, terms, or virtually anything else that departs from your original offer.

It is at this point that negotiations begin in earnest. How well you respond to the seller's counteroffer with your own counter (or acceptance) determines the quality of the deal you'll get.

TIP IT'S THE COUNTER, NOT THE OFFER

Some very savvy buyers will purposely make lowball offers in the hope that the sellers will counter, perhaps at a price lower than the buyer is willing to pay! If not, these savvy buyers hope to engage the sellers in some-times protracted negotiations in the hope of eventually getting a much better price or much better terms.

How Do I Make a Counteroffer?

- You make an offer that the agent and/or attorney writes up.

- The agent presents the offer as soon as possible to the sellers.

- The sellers either accept the offer exactly as presented or turn it down.

- If the sellers turn down the offer, they can make a counteroffer to you. (They can't both accept and counter.)

- You may now accept their counteroffer exactly as written, or turn it down. If you turn it down, you may counter back. (You can't both accept and counter.)

- This countering can go on almost indefinitely. Sometimes it gets down to arguing over a washing machine or repainting one wall of a living room.

- The deal is made only when both you and the seller accept exactly the same counteroffer.

TRAP—YOU CAN'T ACCEPT AND COUNTER

Whenever you or the seller counters with any kind of change at all, it is a new offer. Either party now has the option of walking away from the deal.

Tip 1—The Terrible Offer

Some buyers will purposely make very unfavorable offers to sellers in the hopes they would counter with a compromise offer that was still far below what they were asking. This is a strategy, also called "low-balling" the seller, which sometimes works. However, it is also fraught with peril. Remember, the seller may be insulted by the low offer and simply turn it down out of hand and not counter at all, which could end negotiations. If you accept this risk, however, and the seller does counter, you could be on the way to a great deal.

Tip 2—The Compromise Offer

If you don't want to risk alienating the sellers right off the bat, then there's the compromise offer. It's higher than the lowball, but still far lower than what the seller is asking. This is an offer that you're pretty sure will drive the sellers to the negotiating table. It sets the stage for a bargaining process that will get you the property at a price and terms you can afford and are willing to pay.

How do you know what to put into the "compromise offer?"

What price, terms, and so forth should it be? Every situation is different. However, the general guidelines are that you try to make the lowest offer to which the seller will make a *serious* counter. You'll have to judge the seller's motivation and the market conditions.

Tip 3—The Wonderful Offer

You would only make this offer if you were desperately in love with the home and/or the market was strong. You would offer very close to full price. (Sometimes in a very hot market you might offer full price or higher!)

You want the sellers to know that you're intent on buying their home. But you're hoping that they will cut you a little slack by either accepting your offer as is, or countering by taking a little off the price.

In a normal market, the sellers might indeed accept. Or they might counter, splitting the difference. In a very hot market, they might simply counter by re-offering their original price. Or even offering a higher price than they were asking and than you offered!

Tip 4—Don't Paint Yourself Into a Corner

If you only make terrible offers that favor you, you'll often lose. If you're determined to have the house, you're better off making a counter that contains enough bones for the sellers so that if they don't accept, at least they'll counter back.

Tip 5—Keep the Ball in Play

The goal in bargaining is to keep the ball in play. You always want there to be a counteroffer somewhere en route. The moment either you or the sellers stop countering, the deal is dead.

Tip 6—Pay Attention to Timing

When you make an offer to a seller, it is open ended. That means that you've written down the price, the terms, and any other conditions that you want, and that you agree to be bound by them. If the seller accepts and communicates that acceptance to you, you're on the hook.

However, things change. The house you're in love with today may not be so appealing tomorrow. Yet another home may come along that really turns you on next week. Your financial condition could change. Therefore, you don't want to make this open-ended offer last forever.

Further, if you give the seller lots of time to consider your offer, someone else may slip in a better offer. Therefore, you want to set a strict time limit on your offer and your counters.

Make your offer for as short a time as practical. 24 hours is not unreasonable. Midnight of the day the offer is presented may not be unreasonable, if the sellers can easily be reached. (Be sure to take into consideration how long it will take to contact the sellers. But remember, today, almost everyone is reachable by phone, FAX, or email.)

Tip 7—Don't Let Agents Bully You into Giving More Time

Sometimes agents will encourage you put in a long period of time—four to five days or even a week—for acceptance to take place. They may say that it will take that long to convince the sellers to sign.

This approach makes sense only if the sellers are out of the country, maybe off the planet! Even then it may only be marginally good advice. Remember, the more time the sellers have to think about it, the more time for them to talk themselves out of accepting it. And the more time there is for someone to come in with a better offer. Giving the sellers a lot of time to accept is simply cutting your own throat.

Tip 8—Be Prepared to Withdraw Your Offer

It's important to understand that although your offer is open ended (you're committed; the sellers aren't—until they sign), and although it has a defined time limit for acceptance, you do not have to keep it open. Anytime before the sellers sign *and that acceptance is conveyed to you,* you can withdraw the offer. You make an offer at 5:00 o'clock that the agent will present to the sellers at 8:00 o'clock. At 8:30, you call the sellers' house and ask the agent if they've accepted. He says he's just presented it and they're thinking about it. They'll probably sign in a few minutes. You instruct him to withdraw the offer immediately. The offer is no longer good.

Why would you want to withdraw an offer? There are lots of reasons. Soon after submitting an offer, you find a better house at a better price. You want out of the offer immediately. Or, perish the thought, you or a family member has a car accident or you discover that you have a debilitating disease and you don't want to go through with the deal. Or you're simply being fickle.

It doesn't matter. You don't have to have a reason. You can withdraw the offer anytime before acceptance is communicated to you.

Tip 9—Don't be Confused by Talk That the Sellers Have Accepted Your Offer with a Few Minor Changes

Many first-time buyers are unaware of the important subtleties of unaccepted offers. I have seen agents get sellers to make a counteroffer, then call the buyer and say, "Congratulations—your offer was accepted! Only the seller made a few changes that I'll need to drop by and have you initial. I'll explain it to you when I get there." That's wrong. If the seller changes anything, it's a new offer—totally and completely. A counteroffer is just that. It's a new offer that the seller is making. *You are under no obligation to accept a counteroffer, no matter how close to your original offer it may be.*

Tip 10—Sellers Are Risking, Too

Be aware that sellers are at great risk when they make counteroffers. This is so because they are, in effect, rejecting your offer and substituting another for it. When this happens, the tables are turned. The sellers may give you a time limit to accept their counteroffer and you can do with it what you will. (Just remember, if you counter the counter, once again the ball's in the other court.)

Tip 11—Keep to the Same Document When Possible

It is good strategy to make the counteroffer (either your own or the sellers') on the same document as the original offer. The reason is psychological. When the sellers counter on the same document, even though you may know that their counter rejects your original offer, using the same document makes it somehow seem like you're closer than before. When you counter the sellers' counteroffer, putting it on the same document does the same thing for the seller.

Some agents use sales agreements that have a separate section on the last page that reads, "Seller's Counteroffer." The idea here is that this is the designated place for the sellers to write in their counter.

I think this is a bad idea. It encourages sellers to think that a counteroffer is warranted. A sales agreement with no specific place for the counter, on the other hand, implies that it should be accepted.

Tip 12—Know When to Stop Countering

Sometimes you and the sellers are so far off on price or terms that it becomes obvious that there is no real room for compromise. For example, the best offer you can make is $212,000 and the best counter the seller can make is $250,000. Sometimes you have to accept the fact that not all deals can be made.

Refusing to counter can also be a bargaining tool. After several counteroffers you're still apart on price or terms. Instead of accepting the sellers' most recent counter, you do a "walkaway" and send it back. You include a signed statement to the effect that your last counteroffer (the one before the sellers made their most recent counter) is your final and best offer.

You'll give the sellers until midnight to accept it or you're no longer interested in the property. Further, you're not interested in any more counteroffers from the sellers.

The idea here is to decide the deal on a single throw of the dice. It's all or nothing. You're tired of bargaining. Either the sellers accept what you've offered or you'll go elsewhere.

I've personally used this technique many times and it works for me more often than it fails! You just have to be prepared to give up the house in case the sellers remain adamant.

20

12 Techniques for Helping Your Credit

In today's world, credit is all-important. With good credit you can buy anything, or almost. With good credit you can buy the house of your dreams—a bigger house in a better location on a nicer lot. The problem, of course, is what to do when our credit is not quite what it should be.

Today, being credit challenged does not usually mean you can't get financing. There is undoubtedly a lender out there somewhere who has a loan for everyone. However, the worse your credit, the higher the interest rate, the more cash you must come up with and the lower the LTV (loan-to-value-ratio of the loan to the value of the property). All of which is to say that your ability to afford the home of your dreams, with credit problems, is greatly diminished.

However, there are legitimate ways to improve your credit. Here are 12 techniques that will help both in the long term and in the short run.

Technique 1—Change Your Attitude

Many people are surprised to learn that even a few late payments can seriously affect their ability to get real estate financing. The attitude, "I'll pay when I'm good and ready," may sound defiant against a creditor whom you dislike, but when those late payments show up on your credit report, your future mortgage lender wonders if you'll say the same thing to it.

If you're behind in payments, catch up *before* applying for the mortgage. Try to stay caught up for at least a year before applying so your delinquencies will show up as old rather than recent. Old delinquencies are much easier to forgive.

Technique 2—Verify Your Credit

There are three national credit bureaus: Experion, Transunion, and Equifax. They contain input from many other smaller credit reporting agencies around the country. If you've paid your bills on time, that will show up on this report. And if you haven't paid bills on time and have other problems, that will show up as well. Mortgage lenders regularly order a "three-bureau" report, which sends them your credit from all three. Which is to say, you can't hide bad credit. Therefore, before you apply for a mortgage, probably before you begin house hunting, order a credit report on yourself. (You can do it online; see Online Resources at the back of this book.)

If you find that there are errors, correct them. The credit bureaus will tell you how. If there are problems, see if they can be fixed (see below).

Technique 3—Check Your FICO Score

FICO stands for Fair Isaac and is an independent company that evaluates credit reports by assigning the borrower a numerical rating roughly between 300 and 900. Virtually all lenders use the FICO score. Typically if you score in the high 600s, or higher, you'll get the best financing. Score lower and the financing goes downhill. You can check your FICO score online (see Online Resources at the back of this book) as well as get useful hints on improving it.

Components of Your FICO Score

- Timely repayment of debt (deduct for slow/no payments)
- Foreclosures/bankruptcies (deduct big)

- How much you currently owe (the less the better in relation to how much credit you have—no more than 50 percent on any credit line is good.)
- Your recent applications for credit (more than three in the last six months could be trouble)
- How long you've had your credit cards (the longer—over 10 years—the better)
- Your money management (your history of borrowing wisely)

Technique 4—Improve Your Income/Expense Ratio

You shouldn't fudge, but how you express your income can make a difference. When filling out a mortgage application it usually pays to emphasize length and continuity. For example, you're a teacher who has gotten his first job in years just a month ago. The lender is bound to wonder if you will succeed at the work. However, if you note that you were a teacher with nine years experience a decade ago before leaving the field to help raise children, it can help put your application in a whole new and better light. The lender may be inclined to now count all of your new income instead of just a portion of it.

Technique 5—If You're Self-Employed, Try No-Doc/Low-Doc Loans

How you receive your income is important, too. If you work for an employer and receive wages (meaning a W-2 form at the end of the year), you get preference mainly because it is easy to verify your income and because, presumably, you have something called "job security."

On the other hand, if you're self-employed, you may be turned down. Usually, at minimum you will be asked to produce the last two years of 1040 tax forms. However, in some cases of self-employed individuals, this may not tell the whole story, or you may have been in business for less than two years.

In these cases, ask a mortgage broker about the various no-documentation and low-documentation mortgages out there. You may be able to get the loan based on other factors such as your veracity, money in your account, bank recommendation, and so on.

Technique 6—Pay Off Excess Debt

In calculating how a big a monthly payment/mortgage to give you, lenders take into account your available income. However, the more debt you currently have, the less income is available to pay the new mortgage. Therefore, when possible, pay off as much of your short-term (such as from credit cards) debt as possible. That way you increase your income (less is set aside to pay for the short-term debt) and you may have a better chance of qualifying.

There is a downside to this, however. The more debt you pay off, the less cash you'll have available for a down payment and closing costs. It's really a balancing act.

Technique 7—Put More Money Down

I've emphasized in this book that low-down financing is readily available today—10 percent down, 5 percent down, nothing-down, 103 percent financing. However, to get this requires increasingly better credit.

On the other hand, if your credit isn't wonderful, then you can still get a good low-interest-rate loan if you're able to increase your down payment. Put down 20 percent and lenders will love you. Put down 30 percent, and you should be able to get an equity loan from a lender no matter how bad your credit may be!

Technique 8—Borrow Early for the Down Payment and Closing Costs

Ideally your down payment and closing costs will come from your own funds, earned over the years and set aside as savings. Borrowing the down payment can be a problem. Borrowing the down suggests to the lender that you really can't afford the property. Let the lender know you're borrowing your down payment and you almost certainly will be scuttling the loan.

Therefore, if you need to borrow money that you intend to use as part of the down payment, do it well in advance of applying for the mortgage (at least six months). That way the money will be seen as part of a savings account and the loan will be long established. In other words, you won't be borrowing specifically to make the home purchase.

Gifts for the down payment from relatives also are acceptable today. These must, however, be legitimate gifts. They can't be given with strings attached, such as you'll repay them so much a month and when you sell the property you'll repay the balance in full. In that case they are nothing more than a disguised loan.

Technique 9—Hang onto Old Credit Card Accounts

Lenders want to know that you've been successfully borrowing for a long time. That tells them that you're a good money manager. To determine this they look at your oldest trade lines (credit cards). The older the better.

I've had credit cards for over 20 years. When I recently applied for credit, it was noted that I didn't have long-term cards. Long term meant 30 years or more! Hang onto your old credit cards. Keep a credit card that you've had for years, even if a new credit company offers you a somewhat better deal. That old credit card shows that you have a long history and may help you get your mortgage. This is the case even if you just keep the card in a box and almost never use it!

Technique 10—Don't Have Too Much Credit

Generally speaking, if you apply for credit more than three times within a six-month period, it's likely to be a mark against you. (Yes, it's irrational!) To a lender it looks suspiciously like you may be planning to borrow a lot of money and leave the country.

A good balance between credit cards, car loans, personal finance companies, and other installment loans is best. You don't want a lot of any of these or even a huge total. But the fact that you've got a car loan, three credit cards (a good number), and perhaps a department store card and you've maintained reasonable balances all suggests you're a good credit manager. And that's what the lenders actually want the most.

By the way, don't go to the limit in your credit card charges. It's probably better if you owe half your limit on two cards, rather than your entire limit on one.

Technique 11—Get Bad Credit Fixed

It's a mistaken belief that you can have *all* bad credit "fixed." Companies that offer to fix or make *any* credit problem simply disappear, particularly if they charge you a hefty fee for doing it, may be nothing more than scams.

On the other hand, some types of bad credit can be remedied, either by doing it yourself, or by hiring a company to do it for you. Some of the bad credit that can be fixed includes:

Fixable Bad Credit

- The wrong name, address, social security number, and/or employer
- A creditor's error in reporting a late payment that you made or a continuing loan that you paid off
- A foreclosure that didn't occur or a bankruptcy that never happened

You get the idea. Mistakes and errors can be corrected. But it takes time and effort to do so.

Technique 12—Explain a Problem

If you have a credit problem that can't be fixed, give a logical and coherent explanation for it. If your explanation shows that you at least tried to solve the problem and, perhaps even more important, that the problem was isolated and isn't likely to happen again, you may very well be able to get the financing you want.

The best way to do this is to be up front with the lender. Don't wait for the problem to surface as part of your credit report. Get it out in the open. And provide the lender with a clearly written letter of explanation. If you have late payments because you were ill, but are now well, tell that to the lender. If you were out of work because of a recession, but have now been employed steadily for several years and have paid back your credit problems, explain it. If you had a foreclosure, explain how it occurred and why circumstances are different now.

Your Internet Resources

Government Agencies

Housing and Urban Development *www.hud.gov*
    Information on government programs, including those involving
    settlement/closing procedures

Federal Housing Administration *http://www.hud.gov/offices/hsg/index.cfm*
    Information on FHA loan insurance and housing programs

Veteran's Administration *www.va.gov*
    Information on VA loan guarantees and housing programs

Secondary Lenders

Fannie Mae *www.fanniemae.com* and *www.homepath.com*
    Loans, settlement procedures, and foreclosures

Freddie Mac *www.freddiemac.com*
    Information on loans and settlement procedures

Ginnie Mae *www.ginniemae.gov*
    Information on home purchasing and ownership

Credit Bureaus and Organizations

Consumer Data Industry Associations— *http://www.cdiaonline.org/*
    Information on credit reports and credit laws

Equifax *www.equifax.com*
   National credit reporting agency

Experian *www.experian.com*
   National credit reporting agency

Fair Isaac (credit scores) *www.fairisaac.com*
   Main credit scoring organization

Federal Trade Commission *www.ftc.gov*
   Handles credit reporting complaints

Trans Union *www.transunion.com*
   National credit reporting agency

Title Insurance/Escrow Organizations

ALTA form *www.alta.org/store/forms/homeown.pdf*
   Provides the basic form for ALTA policies

American Escrow Association *http://www.a-e-a.org*
   A major escrow trade association

American Land Title Associations *www.alta.org*
   A major title association trade association

California Escrow Association *www.ceaescrow.org*
   California's trade escrow association

California Land Title Association *www.alta.org/store/forms/homeown.pdf*
   California's trade title association

Chicago Title Insurance Company *www.ctic.com*
   A major title insurance company

First American Title Insurance Company *http://firstam.com*
   Major title insurance company

Illinois Land Title Association *www.illinoislandtitle.org*
   The Illinois trade title insurance association

Texas Land Title Association *www.tlta.com*
   The Texas trade title insurance association

Home Inspection Organizations

American Institute of Inspectors *www.inspection.org*
   A home inspection trade association

American Society of Home Inspectors *www.ashi.com*
  The largest national home inspection trade association

National Association of Certified Home Inspectors *www.nachi.org*
  A national home inspector trade association

Other Related Organizations

Dataquick *www.dataquick.com*
  Provides information on real estate (fee)

National Association of Realtors *www.realtor.com, www.realtor.org.*
  Provides information on members, homes for sale, and other data

Real Estate Services Providers Council www.respro.org
  Provides information on news regarding home closings and other aspects of real estate

The legal description *www.thelegaldescription.com*
  Provides information on legal news regarding home closings

Additional Internet Resource

Robert Irwin *www.robertirwin.com* The author's Web site

Terms You Need to Understand

If you're just getting introduced to real estate, you'll quickly realize that people in this field have a language all their own. There are points and disclosures and contingencies and dozens of other terms that can make you think people are talking in a foreign language.

Since buying a home is one of the biggest financial decisions in life, it's a good idea to become familiar with the following terms, which are frequently used in real estate. All too often a lack of understanding can result in very real consequences such as confusion and failure to act (or inappropriate action) on an important issue.

Abstract of Title

A written document produced by a title insurance company (in some states an attorney will do it) giving the history of who owned the property from the first owner forward. It also indicates any liens or encumbrances that may affect the title. A lender will not make a loan, nor can a sale normally conclude, until the title to real estate is clear, as evidenced by the abstract.

Acceleration Clause

A clause that "accelerates" the payments in a mortgage, meaning that the entire amount becomes immediately due and payable. Most mortgages contain this clause (which kicks in if, for example, you sell the property).

Adjustable Rate Mortgage (ARM)

A mortgage whose interest rate fluctuates according to an index and a margin agreed to in advance by borrower and lender.

Adjustment Date
The day on which an adjustment is made in an adjustable rate mortgage. It may occur monthly, every six months, once a year, or as otherwise agreed.

Agent
Any person licensed to sell real estate, whether a broker or a salesperson.

Alienation Clause
A clause in a mortgage specifying that if the property is transferred to another person, the mortgage becomes immediately due and payable. See also Acceleration Clause.

ALTA
American Land Title Association. A more complete and extensive policy of title insurance and one that most lenders insist upon. It involves a physical inspection and often guarantees the property's boundaries. Lenders often insist on an ALTA policy, with themselves named as beneficiary.

Amortization
Paying back the mortgage in equal installments. In other words, if the mortgage is for 30 years, you pay in 360 equal installments. (The last payment is often a few dollars more or less. This is the opposite of a Balloon Payment, which is a payment that is considerably larger than the rest.) See Balloon Payment.

Annual Percentage Rate (APR)
The rate paid for a loan, including interest, loan fees, and points as determined by a government formula.

Appraisal
Valuation of a property, usually by a qualified appraiser, as required by most lenders. The amount of the appraisal is the maximum value on which the loan will be based. For example, if the appraisal is $100,000 and the lender loans 80 percent of value, the maximum mortgage will be $80,000.

ASA
American Society of Appraisers. A professional organization of appraisers.

As Is
A property sold without warrantees from the sellers. The sellers are essentially saying that they won't make any repairs.

Assignment of Mortgage
The lender's sale of a mortgage usually without the borrower's permission. For example, you may obtain a mortgage from XYZ Savings and Loan, which then sells the mortgage to Bland Bank. You will get a letter saying that the mortgage was assigned and you are to make your payments to a new entity. The document used between lenders for the transfer is the "assignment of mortgage."

Assumption
Taking over an existing mortgage. For example, a seller may have an assumable mortgage on a property. When you buy the property, you take over that seller's obligation under the loan. Today most fixed rate mortgages are not assumable.

Most adjustable rate mortgages are assumable, but the borrower must qualify. FHA and VA mortgages may be assumable if certain conditions are met. When you assume the mortgage, you may be personally liable if there is a foreclosure.

Automatic Guarantee
The power assigned to some lenders to guarantee VA loans without first checking with the Veterans Administration. These lenders can often make the loans more quickly.

Backup
An offer that comes in after an earlier offer is accepted. If both buyer and seller agree, the backup assumes a secondary position to be acted upon only if the original deal does not go through.

Balloon Payment
A single mortgage payment, usually the last, that is larger than all the others. In the case of second mortgages held by sellers, often

only interest is paid until the due date—then the entire amount borrowed (the principal) is due. See Second Mortgage.

Biweekly Mortgage
A mortgage that is paid every other week instead of monthly.
Since there are 52 weeks in the year, you end up making 26 payments, or the equivalent of one month's extra payment. The additional payments, applied to the principal, significantly reduce the amount of interest charged on the mortgage and often reduce the term of the loan.

Blanket Mortgage
A mortgage that covers several properties instead of a single property. It is used most frequently by developers and builders.

Broker
An independent licensed agent, one who can establish his or her own office. Salespeople, although they are licensed, must work for brokers, typically for a few years, to get enough experience to become licensed as brokers.

Buy-Down Mortgage
A mortgage with a lower than market interest rate, either for the entire term of the mortgage or for a set period at the beginning—say, two years. The buy-down is made possible by the builder or seller paying an up-front fee to the lender.

Buyer's Agent
A real estate agent whose loyalty is to the buyer and not to the seller. Such agents are becoming increasingly common today.

Call Provision
A clause in a mortgage allowing the lender to call in the entire unpaid balance of the loan providing certain events have occurred, such as sale of the property.
See also Acceleration Clause.

Canvass
To work a neighborhood, to go through it, and knock on every door. Agents canvass to find listings. Investors and home buyers do it to

find potential sellers who have not yet listed their property—and may agree to sell quickly for less.

Caps
Limits put on an adjustable rate mortgage. The interest rate, the monthly payment, or both may be capped.

CC&Rs
Covenants, conditions, and restrictions. These limit the activities you as an owner may do. For example, you may be required to seek approval of a Home Owners' Association before adding on or changing the color of your house. Or you may be restricted from adding a second or third story to your home.

Certificate of Reasonable Value (CRV)
A document issued by the Veterans Administration establishing what the VA feels is the property's maximum value. In some cases, if a buyer pays more than this amount for the property, he or she will not get the VA loan.

Chain of Title
The history of ownership of the property. The title to property forms a chain going back to the first owners, which in the Southwest, for example, may come from original Spanish land grants.

Closing
When the seller conveys title to the buyer and the buyer makes full payment, including financing, for the property. At the closing, all required documents are signed and delivered and funds are disbursed.

Commission
The fee charged for an agent's services. Usually, but not always, the seller pays. There is no "set" fee; rather, the amount is fully negotiable.

Commitment
A promise from lender to borrower offering a mortgage at a set amount, interest rate, and cost. Typically, commitments have a time limit—for example, they are good for 5 or 15 days. Some lenders charge for making a commitment if you don't subsequently take out

the mortgage (since they have tied up the money for that amount of time). When the lender's offer is in writing, it is sometimes called a "firm commitment."

Conforming Loan
A mortgage that conforms to the underwriting requirements of Fannie Mae or Freddie Mac.

Construction Loan
A mortgage made for the purpose of constructing a building. The loan is short term, typically under 12 months, and is usually paid in installments directly to the builder as the work is completed. Most often, it is interest only.

Contingency
A condition that limits a contract. For example, the most common contingency says that a buyer is not required to complete a purchase if he or she fails to get necessary financing. See also Subject To.

Conventional Loan
Any loan that is not guaranteed or insured by the government.

Convertible Mortgage
An adjustable rate mortgage (ARM) with a clause allowing it to be converted to a fixed rate mortgage at some time in the future. You may have to pay an additional cost to obtain this type of mortgage.

Cosigner
Someone with better credit (usually a close relative) who agrees to sign your loan if you do not have good enough credit to qualify for a mortgage. The cosigner is equally responsible for repayment of the loan. (If you don't pay it back, the cosigner can be held liable for the entire balance.)

Credit Report
A report, usually from one of the country's three large credit reporting companies, that gives your credit history. It typically lists all your delinquent payments or failures to pay as well as any bankruptcies and, sometimes, foreclosures. Lenders use the report to determine

whether to offer you a mortgage. The fee for obtaining the report is usually under $50, and you are charged for it.

Deal Point
A point on which the deal hinges. It can be as important as the price or as trivial as changing the color of the mailbox.

Deposit
The money that buyers put up (also called "earnest money") to demonstrate their seriousness in making an offer. The deposit is usually at risk if the buyers fail to complete the transaction and have no acceptable way of backing out of the deal.

Disclosures
A list and explanation of features and defects in a property that sellers give to buyers. Most states now require disclosures.

Discount
The amount that a lender withholds from a mortgage to cover the points and fees. For example, you may borrow $100,000, but your points and fees come to $3000; hence the lender will fund only $97,000, discounting the $3000. Also, in the secondary market, a discount is the amount less than face value that a buyer of a mortgage pays in order to be induced to take out the loan. The discount here is calculated on the basis of risk, market rates, interest rate of the note, and other factors. See Points.

Dual Agent
An agent who expresses loyalty to both buyers and sellers and agrees to work with both. Only a few agents can successfully play this role.

Due-on-Encumbrance Clause
A little noted and seldom-enforced clause in recent mortgages that allows the lender to foreclose if the borrower gets additional financing.

For example, if you secure a second mortgage, the lender of the first mortgage may have grounds for foreclosing. The reasoning here is that if you reduce your equity level by taking out additional financing, the lender may be placed in a less secure position.

246

Due-on-Sale Clause
A clause in a mortgage specifying that the entire unpaid balance becomes due and payable on sale of the property. See Acceleration Clause.

Escrow Company
An independent third party (stakeholder) that handles funds; carries out the instructions of the lender, buyer, and seller in a transaction; and deals with all the documents. In most states, companies are licensed to handle escrows. In some parts of the country, particularly the Northeast, the function of the escrow company may be handled by an attorney.

FHA Loan
A mortgage insured by the Federal Housing Administration. In most cases, the FHA advances no money, but instead insures the loan to a lender such as a bank.

There is a fee to the borrower, usually paid up front, for this insurance.

Fixed Rate Mortgage
A mortgage whose interest rate does not fluctuate for the life of the loan.

Fixer-Upper
A home that does not show well and is in bad shape. Often the property is euphemistically referred to in listings as a "TLC" (needs tender loving care) or "handyman's special."

Foreclosure
Legal proceeding in which the lender takes possession and title to a property, usually after the borrower fails to make timely payments on a mortgage.

Fannie Mae
Any of the publicly traded securities collateralized by a pool of mortgages backed by the Federal National Mortgage Association. A secondary lender.

Freddie Mac
A publicly traded security collateralized by a pool of mortgages backed by the Federal Home Loan Mortgage Corporation: A secondary lender.

FSBO
For sale by owner.

Garbage Fees
Extra (and often unnecessary) charges tacked on when a buyer obtains a mortgage.

Graduated-Payment Mortgage
A mortgage whose payments vary over the life of the loan. They start out low, then slowly rise until, usually after a few years, they reach a plateau where they remain for the balance of the term. Such a mortgage is particularly useful when you want low initial payments. It is primarily used by first-time buyers, often in combination with a fixed rate or adjustable rate mortgage.

Growing Equity Mortgage
A rarely used mortgage whose payments increase according to a set schedule. The purpose is to pay additional money into principal and thus pay off the loan earlier and save interest charges.

HOA
Homeowners' Association, found mainly in condos but also in some single-family areas. It represents homeowners and establishes and maintains neighborhood architectural and other standards. You usually must get permission from the HOA to make significant external changes to your property.

Index
A measurement of an established interest rate used to determine the periodic adjustments for adjustable rate mortgages. There are a wide variety of indexes, including the Treasury bill rates and the cost of funds to lenders.

Inspection
A physical survey of the property to determine if there are any problems or defects.

Jumbo
A mortgage for more than the maximum amount of a Conforming Loan.

Lien
A claim for money against real estate. For example, if you had work done on your property and refused to pay the worker, he or she might file a "mechanic's lien" against your property. If you didn't pay taxes, the taxing agency might file a "tax lien." These liens "cloud" the title and usually prevent you from selling the property or refinancing it until they are cleared by paying off the debt.

Loan-to-Value Ratio (LTV)
The percentage of the appraised value of a property that a lender will loan. For example, if your property appraises at $100,000 and the lender is willing to loan $80,000, the loan-to-value ratio is 80 percent.

Lock In
To tie up the interest rate for a mortgage in advance of actually getting it. For example, a buyer might "lock in" a mortgage at 7.5 percent so that if rates subsequently rose, he or she would still get that rate. Sometimes there's a fee for this. It's always a good idea to get it in writing from the lender, just to be sure that if rates rise the lender doesn't change its mind.

Lowball
To make a very low initial offer to purchase.

MAI
Member, American Institute of Real Estate Appraisers. An appraiser with this designation has completed rigorous training.

Margin
An amount, calculated in points, that a lender adds to an index to determine how much interest you will pay during a period for an

adjustable rate mortgage. For example, the index may be at 7 percent and the margin, agreed upon at the time you obtain the mortgage, may be 2.7 points. The interest rate for that period, therefore, is 9.7 percent. See also Index, Points.

Median Sales Price

The midpoint of the price of homes—as many properties have sold above this price as have sold below it.

MLS

Multiple Listing Service—used by Realtors as a listings exchange. Nearly 90 percent of all homes listed in the country are found on the MLS.

Mortgage

A loan arrangement between a borrower, or "mortgagor," and a lender, or "mortgagee." If you don't make your payments on a mortgage, the lender can foreclose, or take ownership of the property, only by going to court. This court action can take a great deal of time, often six months or more. Further, even after the lender has taken back the property, you may have an "equity of redemption" that allows you to redeem the property for years afterward, by paying back the mortgage and the lender's costs.

The length of time it takes to foreclose, the costs involved, and the equity of redemption make a mortgage much less desirable to lenders than a Trust Deed.

Mortgage Banker

A lender that specializes in offering mortgages but none of the other services normally provided by a bank.

Mortgage Broker

A company that specializes in providing "retail" mortgages to consumers.

It usually represents many different lenders.

Motivated Seller

A seller who has a strong desire to sell. For example, the seller may have been transferred and must move quickly.

Multiple Counteroffers
Comeback offers extended by the seller to several buyers simultaneously.

Multiple Offers
Offers submitted simultaneously from several buyers for the same property.

Negative Amortization
A condition arising when the payment on an adjustable rate mortgage is not sufficiently large to cover the interest charged. The excess interest is then added to the principal, so that the amount borrowed actually increases. The amount that the principal can increase is usually limited to 125 percent of the original mortgage value. Any mortgage that includes payment caps has the potential to be negatively amortized.

Origination Fee
An expense in obtaining a mortgage. Originally, it was a charge that lenders made for preparing and submitting a mortgage. The fee applied only to FHA and VA loans, which had to be submitted to the government for approval. With an FHA loan, the maximum origination fee was 1 percent.

Personal Property
Any property that does not go with the land. Such property includes automobiles, clothing, and most furniture. Some items such as appliances and floor and wall coverings are disputable. See also Real Property.

PITI
Principal, interest, taxes, and insurance. These are the major components that go into determining the monthly payment on a mortgage. (Other items include homeowner's dues and utilities.)

Points
A point is 1 percent of a mortgage amount, payable on obtaining the loan. For example, if your mortgage is $100,000 and you are

required to pay 2½ points to get it, the charge to you is $2500. Some points may be tax deductible. Check with your accountant.

A "basis point" is 1100 of a point. For example, if you are charged 12 point (0.5 percent of the mortgage), the lender may refer to it as 50 basis points.

Preapproval
Formal approval for a mortgage from a lender. You have to submit a standard application and have a credit check. Also, the lender may require proof of income, employment, and money on deposit (to be used for the down payment and closing costs).

Prepayment Penalty
A charge demanded by the lender from the borrower for paying off a mortgage early. In times past (more than 25 years ago) nearly all mortgages carried prepayment penalties. However, those mortgages were also assumable by others. Today virtually no fixed rate mortgages (other than FHA or VA mortgages) are truly assumable, however some carry a prepayment penalty clause. See Assumption.

Private Mortgage Insurance (PMI)
Insurance that protects the lender in the event that the borrower defaults on a mortgage. It is written by an independent third-party insurance company and typically covers only the first 20 percent of the lender's potential loss. PMI is normally required on any mortgage that exceeds an 80 percent loan-to-value ratio.

Purchase Money Mortgage
A mortgage obtained as part of the purchase price of a home (usually from the seller), as opposed to a mortgage obtained through refinancing.

In some states, no deficiency judgment can be obtained against the borrower of a purchase money mortgage. (That is, if there is a foreclosure and the property brings less than the amount borrowed, the borrower cannot be held liable for the shortfall.)

Real Property
Real estate. This includes the land and anything appurtenant to it, including the house. Certain tests have been devised to determine

whether an item is real property (goes with the land). For example, if curtains or drapes have been attached in such a way that they cannot be removed without damaging the home, they may be spoken of as real property. On the other hand, if they can easily be removed without damaging the home, they may be personal property. The purchase agreement should specify whether doubtful items are real or personal to avoid confusion later on.

Realtor®
A broker who is a member of the National Association of Realtors. Agents who are not members may not use the Realtor designation.

REO
Real estate owned—a term that refers to property taken back through foreclosure and held for sale by a lender.

RESPA
Real Estate Settlement Procedures Act. Legislation requiring lenders to provide borrowers with specified information on the cost of securing financing. Basically it means that before you proceed far along the path of getting the mortgage, the lender has to provide you with an estimate of costs. Then, before you sign the documents binding you to the mortgage, the lender has to provide you with a breakdown of the actual costs.

Second Mortgage
An inferior mortgage usually placed on the property after a first mortgage. In the event of foreclosure, the second mortgage is paid off only if and when the first mortgage had been fully paid. Many lenders will not offer second mortgages.

Short Sale
Property sale in which a lender agrees to accept less than the mortgage amount in order to facilitate the sale and avoid a foreclosure.

SREA
Society of Real Estate Appraisers—a professional association to which qualified appraisers can belong.

Subject To
A phrase often used to indicate that a buyer is not assuming the mortgage liability of a seller. For example, if the seller has an assumable loan and you (the buyer) "assume" the loan, you are taking over liability for payment. On the other hand, if you purchase "subject to" the mortgage, you do not assume liability for payment.

Subordination Clause
A clause in a mortgage document that keeps the mortgage subordinate to another mortgage.

Title
Legal evidence that you actually have the right of ownership of Real Property. It is given in the form of a deed (there are many different types of deeds) that specifies the kind of title you have (joint, common, or other).

Title Insurance Policy
An insurance policy that covers the title to a home. It may list the owner or the lender as beneficiary. The policy is issued by a title insurance company and specifies that if for any covered reason your title proves defective, the company will correct the title or compensate you up to a specified amount, usually the amount of the purchase price or the mortgage.

Trust Deed
A three-party lending arrangement that includes a borrower, or "trustor;" an independent third-party stakeholder, or "trustee" (usually a title insurance company); and a lender, or "beneficiary" so-called because the lender stands to benefit if the trustee turns the deed over in case the borrower fails to make payments. The advantage of the trust deed over the mortgage is that foreclosure can be accomplished without court action or deficiency judgment against the borrower. (In other words, if the property is worth less than the loan, the lender can't come back to the borrower after the sale for the difference.) See also Purchase Money Mortgage.

Upgrade

Any extra that a buyer may obtain when purchasing a new home—for example, a better-quality carpet or a wall mirror in the bedroom.

Upside Down

Owing more on a property than its market value.

VA Loan

A mortgage guaranteed by the Veterans Administration. The VA actually guarantees only a small percentage of the loan amount, but since it guarantees the "top" of the monies loaned, lenders are willing to accept the arrangement. In a VA loan the government advances no money; rather, the mortgage is made by a private lender such as a bank.

Wraparound Financing

A blend of two mortgages, often used by sellers to get a higher interest rate or facilitate a sale. For example, instead of giving a buyer a simple Second Mortgage, the seller may combine the balance due on an existing mortgage (usually an existing first) with an additional loan. Thus the wrap includes both the second and the first mortgages. The borrower makes payments to the seller, who then keeps part of the payment and in turn pays off the existing mortgage.

Index